Your Prayers Matter

Geary Reid

ISBN: 978-976-8305-28-2

Acknowledgements

Great thanks must be expressed to the following people:

The heavenly Father, for granting me the wisdom and inspiration to record the information in this book, which I began on October 28, 2020, and completed on November 5, 2020; my family, for their continued encouragement and support regarding various challenges; and several people who have assisted with reviewing and editing the book:

- Wonnette Nicholson, Dipl. in Business Management and Administration
- Rev. Rickford Fanfair
- Shawn Rogers, Adv. Dipl. Project Mgmt., A+ Certification, Telecommunication Certification
- Roxanne Abrams-Ramprashad

To you, the reader: have fun while reading, and grasp and practice what you learn so that this world will become a better place. Many people are depending on your guidance. We all need a shoulder to lean on and a hand to guide us.

Rev. Geary Reid
MBA, FCCA, FAAPM, MPM, CAT

Reid's Learning Institute and Business Consultancy

reidnlearn.com

Amazon: amazon.com/author/gearyreid

Facebook: Reid n Learn

Instagram: Reid n Learn

LinkedIn: Reid's Learning Institute and Business Consultancy

199 Kuru - Kururu, Soesdyke Linden Highway
Guyana, South America

Table of contents

Introduction

Praying is not optional for the believer; it must become a lifestyle, where every believer constantly seeks the presence of the Lord for their breakthrough and success. Their prayer may not be answered at their first request, but they must not give up easily.

Prayer is so important that Jesus taught his disciples to pray. When Jesus walked on the earth, he knew that he was going to be crucified, yet he prayed before his crucifixion. If Jesus, who is the Son of God, spends time praying, why would believers think that they ought not to pray daily? Before Jesus started his earthly ministry, he fasted forty days and nights so that he would be empowered and God the Father would be with him throughout his short journey on the earth.

Every believer must remember that if they want to be effective in their prayer, they must forgive people. Unforgiveness hinders prayer. Fasting is another important ingredient in every believer's prayer life and must be done frequently.

No believer must accept poverty, since God wants all saints to prosper. Satan plans to keep the believers poor, but every believer must pray that God will make them prosperous. Those who are poor will know that they have to be diligent in what they are doing so that God will bless their hands.

Everyone must pray: men, women, children, and families. God has many things available to believers, but if they do not pray, nothing will happen.

There are many mountains that stand before a person's life, but with prayer, those mountains will be removed. Prayer is so powerful that it will open prison doors that were secured. God will always protect his children and provide ways of escape for them.

Rain is seen as part of nature, but when believers pray, they can shut up the heavens from raining, and when they pray again, they can command the rain to return. Besides rain, believers can also call down the fire of God to destroy the works of darkness.

Those who are sick have access to God's healing power, and the elders in the church have a responsibility to pray for those who need God's healing. Those who are demon-possessed can be delivered through the power of prayer. When persons are barren, they ought not to blame each other, but seek God for deliverance from barrenness.

The gospel has to reach all parts of the earth; therefore, believers must pray that God enlarges their borders. They must seek God so that he will give them favor in every area of their lives. If you have prayed and have not seen any results, then pray and pray until God gives you the victory. Prayer is a key with the potential to unlock many doors without human confrontation. Nothing is too difficult when prayer becomes part of your equation, along with God's favor.

1. Forgiveness

God intends for everyone to pray. However, he does not want anyone to approach him with a dirty heart. A dirty heart prevents the flow of information from the believer unto God. A dirty heart operates like a clogged sink pipe, which prevents the free flow of water.

Therefore, those who are praying to God have a responsibility to cleanse their hearts. If they fail to cleanse their hearts, they are only hindering their future.

1.1 A clean heart

David had sinned against God. He wanted God to hear his prayer, but he knew that he had to cleanse his heart. Therefore, before he made his request to God, he chose to ask God to cleanse his heart.

The approach taken by David must be taken by every believer. While David's sins are well known in the Bible, those who sin in other ways also need God to cleanse their hearts.

Psalm 51:1-12

[1] Have mercy upon me, O God, according to thy lovingkindness: according unto the multitude of thy tender mercies blot out my transgressions. [2] Wash me thoroughly from mine iniquity, and cleanse me from my sin. [3] For I acknowledge my transgressions: and my sin is ever before me. [4] Against thee, thee only, have I sinned, and done this evil in thy sight: that thou mightest be justified when thou speakest, and be clear when thou judgest.

[5] Behold, I was shaped in iniquity; and in sin did my mother conceive me. [6] Behold, thou desirest truth in the inward parts: and in the hidden part thou shalt make me to know wisdom. [7] Purge me with hyssop, and I shall be clean: wash me, and I shall be whiter than snow.

[8] Make me to hear joy and gladness; that the bones which thou hast broken may rejoice. [9] Hide thy face from my sins, and blot out all mine iniquities.

[10] Create in me a clean heart, O God; and renew a right spirit within me. [11] Cast me not away from thy presence; and take not thy holy spirit from me. [12] Restore unto me the joy of thy salvation; and uphold me with thy free spirit.

As David continued his plea before God, he said in Psalm 51:4 that it was only God that he had sinned against. He is correct, because when a person sins, they do not sin against other people. Since David knew that he had sinned against God, he went to God for the cleansing of his heart.

A few questions for all believers:

- How many of us know that we have sinned?
- How many of us know that we have sinned against God?
- How long will we live in our sins?
- How many of us know that we have to seek God's forgiveness?

Figure 1. Why believers need a clean heart

(All figures developed by the author unless otherwise noted.)

Every believer must desire that God hears their prayers. When believers are confronted with problems, they must be able to talk to God and immediately receive his protection and blessing. However, if their heart is not clean, then their prayer will not be heard by God.

Too many believers are busy expending energy on other things, and their prayers are not heard. Therefore, they must do like David, according to Psalm 51:1-12, and cleanse their hearts, so that their prayers will be heard and answered.

1.2 Remove hatred

Believers must cleanse their hearts of many things. One such thing is hatred. No one can expect God to hear their prayer if they hate their brother and sister. While some persons feel that no one is looking, they must remember that God is omnipresent, so he is always looking at them. Man often sees the outer part of persons, but God sees the heart. No amount of clothes can prevent God from seeing the heart.

1 John 1:6-10

[6] If we say that we have fellowship with him, and walk in darkness, we lie, and do not the truth: [7] But if we walk in the light, as he is in the light, we have fellowship one with another, and the blood of Jesus Christ his Son cleanseth us from all sin. [8] If we say that we have no sin, we deceive ourselves, and the truth is not in us. [9] If we confess our sins, he is faithful and just to forgive us our sins, and to cleanse us from all unrighteousness. [10] If we say that we have not sinned, we make him a liar, and his word is not in us.

Take note of 1 John 1:8-9, which tells us no one can say that they are free from sin. Therefore, everyone must seek forgiveness. It shows that God is willing and able to forgive any one of their sins, if they approach him with a repentant heart. Therefore, no one has an excuse to keep sin in their heart.

1.3 Forgive those on earth their sins

Many persons want to have a good relationship with God but refuse to forgive their brothers or sisters of their sins. Jesus provides a sharp reminder to every believer that before they approach the Father in prayer, they must go and forgive those whom they have hurt. This is a tough lesson, but it helps everyone to make their relationship right with people.

Matthew 18:15-19

[15] Moreover if thy brother shall trespass against thee, go and tell him his fault between thee and him alone: if he shall hear thee, thou hast gained thy brother. [16] But if he will not hear thee, then take with thee one or two more, that in the mouth of two or three witnesses every word may be established. [17] And if he shall neglect to hear them, tell it unto the church: but if he neglect to hear the church, let him be unto thee as an heathen man and a publican. [18] Verily I say unto you, Whatsoever ye shall bind on earth shall be bound in heaven: and whatsoever ye shall loose on earth shall be loosed in heaven. [19] Again I say unto you, that if two of you shall agree on earth as touching any thing that they shall ask, it shall be done for them of my Father which is in heaven.

God wants every believer to approach him with their prayers, but he hates when they harbor bitterness in their hearts. When believers refuse to forgive persons, they are only wasting their time by bringing their gifts to the altar. Those who seek to forgive must be genuine. Also, when someone seeks to forgive, the other person must be willing to accept the forgiveness offered to them.

Figure 2. Forgive yourself and others, and God will forgive you

Some persons believe that because of the magnitude of some offenses, they must not forgive the offender, even if that person approaches them and asks forgiveness. But God sees sin as sin. Therefore, God wants all those who sin to seek forgiveness.

1.4 God is waiting for you to forgive others

Some persons think that they can approach God with sin in their hearts and that God will hear them. However, they are once again reminded that when they forgive persons for their sins, then God will forgive them for their sins. Therefore, God is waiting for persons to approach him and confess their sins, and then he will hear their prayer.

Figure 3. Forgiveness starts with God and must be continued by all believers

Mark 11:25-26

[25] And when ye stand praying, forgive, if ye have ought against any: that your Father also which is in heaven may forgive you your trespasses. [26] But if ye do not forgive, neither will your Father which is in heaven forgive your trespasses.

1.5 Believers must seek peaceful forgiveness

Seeking forgiveness must not be confrontational. It must be done in love and peace as believers.

Figure 4. Believers seeking peaceful forgiveness

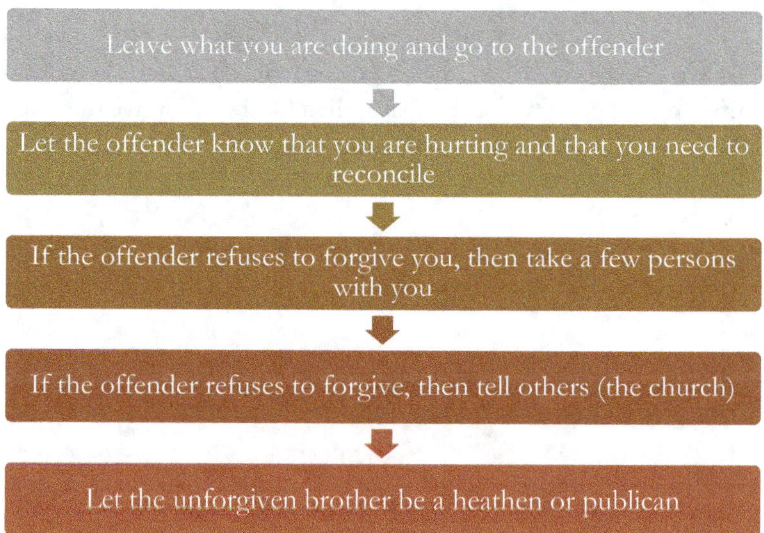

When a person refuses to forgive others, they may not recognize that God is not listening to them. They may think that they have to fast and pray, but that will not cause God to take any action except to remind them that they must forgive others.

Figure 5. Forgive people and God will bless you

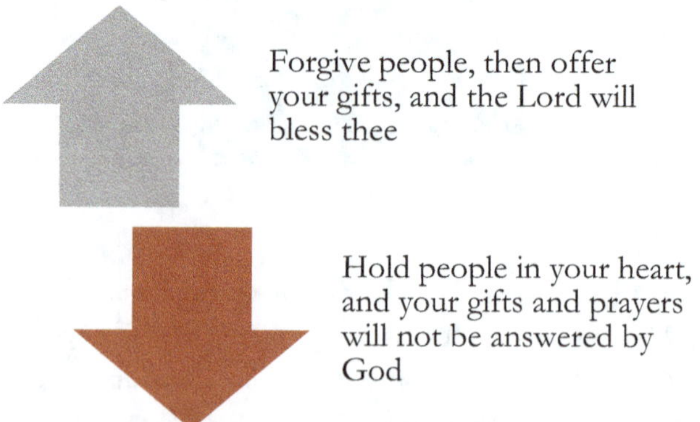

When Jesus was teaching his disciples to pray, he included the element of forgiveness. Many persons may wonder why he had to tell them to forgive others, but those who refuse to forgive will be hindering their progress.

Matthew 6:11-12

[11] Give us this day our daily bread. [12] And forgive us our debts, as we forgive our debtors.

Those who refuse to forgive are only making life difficult for themselves. The longer they take to forgive persons their sins, the more they are creating a brick wall between themselves and God.

Figure 6. Unforgiveness creates a brick wall

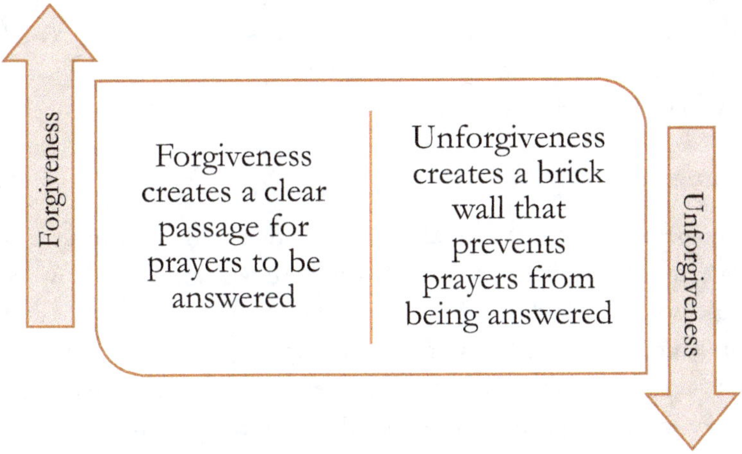

2. Fasting

Prayer by itself is good, and everyone must pray. However, fasting is also important, and every believer must be willing to fast and make their request known unto the Lord.

People believe that they have to make too much sacrifice when they fast. However, their sacrifice is often evident with great results. Fasting requires persons to abstain from something. As they abstain, they are strengthening their relationship with the Lord, and knowing God is a great rewarder for those who make sacrifices for him.

2.1 When to fast?

Some people have established in their minds that they will only fast when they have problems, or when they need something from God. However, that is not the way that God wants his children to approach him. He wants them to be in a mode of regular fasting and praying.

The same way persons will make prayer and praise a lifestyle, they must also make fasting a lifestyle. Adopting this lifestyle gives them closer access to God's presence so that he swiftly answers their prayer.

Figure 7. Possible times to fast

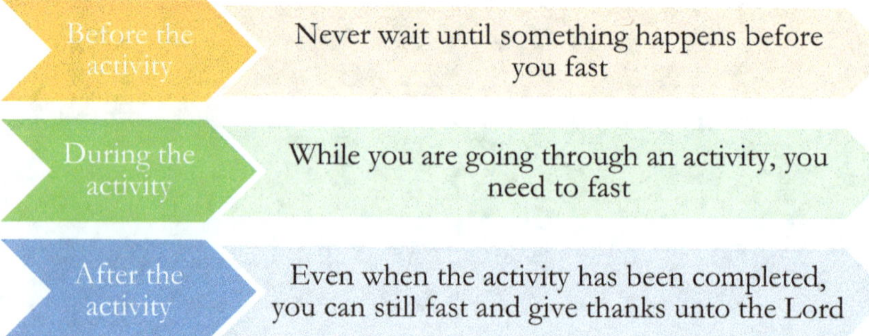

There are times when a person gets a victory, and in rejoicing, they sometimes forget God and begin to think that they gave themselves that victory. However, when they continue to pray and praise God after the activity, they give Satan no room to have victory over their lives.

2.2 Fasting is a private matter

When some persons are about to fast, they will make a public announcement about it to everyone they know or come into contact with. However, Jesus was quick to address this matter and encourage persons to remain simple when they fast. Their fasting is a matter between them and God.

Matthew 6:16-18

[16] Moreover when ye fast, be not, as the hypocrites, of a sad countenance: for they disfigure their faces, that they may appear unto men to fast. Verily I say unto you, They have their reward. [17] But thou, when thou fastest, anoint thine head, and wash thy face; [18] That thou appear not unto men to fast, but unto thy Father which is in secret: and thy Father, which seeth in secret, shall reward thee openly.

If a person wants to fast but also wants to draw the attention of others, then they are only getting into vain actions. It is never God's intention that persons try to draw attention to themselves when they fast.

Figure 8. Comparison of hypocrites and believers fasting (Matthew 6:16-18)

Hypocrites fasting	Believers fasting
Sad countenance	Anoint their head (giving God the opportunity to come into their lives)
Disfigure their faces	Wash their face (an act of removing sins from their lives and keeping themselves looking fresh)

When the hypocrites fast, they will be known by people. This happens because most of what they do are outward things, according to Matthew 6:16. However, Jesus advises believers not to be involved in events that draw public attention. When the public is less involved, it gives the believers more time to concentrate on God and what he will do for them.

Figure 9. Who rewards hypocrites and believers for their fasting?

The rewards from God are long-lasting, while the rewards from people are temporal and cannot deliver a person. Everyone who needs God's intervention needs to seek him when they are fasting and move away from seeking people's acknowledgment.

2.3 Who should fast?

Some persons believe that only selected persons should fast. However, all those who are physically and mentally alert should be involved in fasting. There may be some persons who can be excluded from fasting for various reasons. For example, some elderly persons may not fast, due to aging and/or medical issues.

Figure 10. Possible persons who can be excluded from fasting

Pregnant women

Physically sick

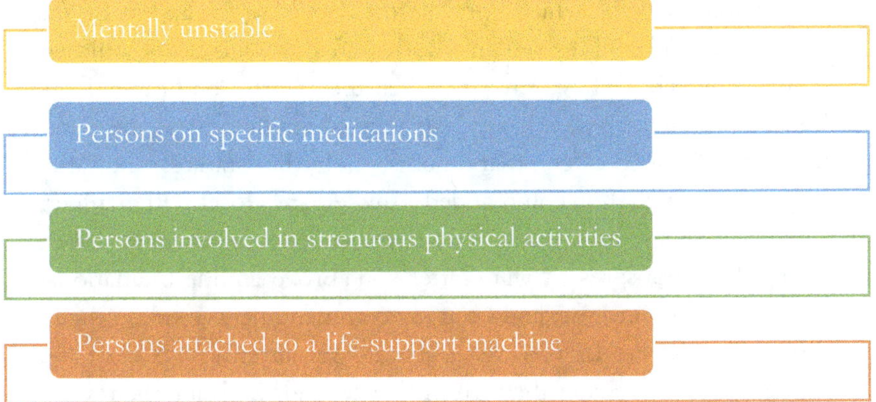

Those who are involved in fasting must know that they are doing something beneficial for themselves. While they have to make sacrifices, they can look forward to great success.

2.4 Fast before engaging in activities

There is an important lesson to learn from Nehemiah. He heard what had happened in the captivity of the people of God. He wanted to rebuild the wall of the Lord, so he fasted and prayed for direction. This is something that all believers must do.

Nehemiah 1:1-10

[1] The words of Nehemiah the son of Hachaliah. And it came to pass in the month Chisleu, in the twentieth year, as I was in Shushan the palace, [2] that Hanani, one of my brethren, came, he and certain men of Judah; and I asked them concerning the Jews that had escaped, which were left of the captivity, and concerning Jerusalem. [3] And they said unto me, The remnant that are left of the captivity there in the province are in great affliction and reproach: the wall of Jerusalem also is broken down, and the gates thereof are burned with fire.

[4] And it came to pass, when I heard these words, that I sat down and wept, and mourned certain days, and fasted, and prayed before the God of heaven, [5] And said, I beseech thee, O LORD God of heaven, the great and terrible God, that keepeth covenant and mercy for them that love him and observe his commandments: [6] Let thine ear now be attentive, and thine eyes open, that thou mayest hear the

prayer of thy servant, which I pray before thee now, day and night, for the children of Israel thy servants, and confess the sins of the children of Israel, which we have sinned against thee: both I and my father's house have sinned. [7] We have dealt very corruptly against thee, and have not kept the commandments, nor the statutes, nor the judgments, which thou commandedst thy servant Moses. [8] Remember, I beseech thee, the word that thou commandedst thy servant Moses, saying, If ye transgress, I will scatter you abroad among the nations: [9] But if ye turn unto me, and keep my commandments, and do them; though there were of you cast out unto the uttermost part of the heaven, yet will I gather them from thence, and will bring them unto the place that I have chosen to set my name there. [10] Now these are thy servants and thy people, whom thou hast redeemed by thy great power, and by thy strong hand.

In verse 4, Nehemiah decided to fast and pray because the walls of Jerusalem were broken down and the gates were burnt. This showed that this servant had a great concern for the things of God. He took the destruction of the Jerusalem walls and gate and made it his concern, and he prayed about the matter. After he got God's approval, then he proceeded to rebuild the wall. Although believers have to work for the Lord, they must put their matter to God in prayer and fasting, since they need God to sanction their work.

3. Prayer for prosperity

God intends to make everyone prosperous. Therefore, those who are not prospering need to pray for their prosperity.

Throughout the Bible, there are many reminders of God wanting his people to prosper. He is a loving God who wants the best for his children.

Matthew 6:33

33 But seek ye first the kingdom of God, and his righteousness; and all these things shall be added unto you.

Those who seek God can expect that he will make them prosperous. Believers ought not to be poor. Therefore, they must know that God is on their side.

1 Chronicles 22:11-13

11 Now, my son, the LORD be with thee; and prosper thou, and build the house of the LORD thy God, as he hath said of thee. 12 Only the LORD give thee wisdom and understanding, and give thee charge concerning Israel, that thou mayest keep the law of the LORD thy God. 13 Then shalt thou prosper, if thou takest heed to fulfil the statutes and judgments which the LORD charged Moses with concerning Israel: be strong, and of good courage; dread not, nor be dismayed.

Prosperity does not require persons to do things that are outside the requirements of God. Humans must be willing to obey, pray, and serve the Lord, and let God cause them to prosper.

Job 36:11-12

[11] If they obey and serve him, they shall spend their days in prosperity, and their years in pleasures. [12] But if they obey not, they shall perish by the sword, and they shall die without knowledge.

3.1 Believe when you pray

As persons desire to be prosperous, they must pray and believe. If persons doubt when they pray, they will nullify their prayer. Therefore, they must believe that what they prayed for will become possible.

Mark 11:24

[24] Therefore I say unto you, what things soever ye desire, when ye pray, believe that ye receive them, and ye shall have them.

3.2 Be specific when you are praying

Those who want prosperity must be specific in their prayer, and they should also assign a timeline to it. Too many persons pray vague prayers and expect God to work on their behalf. God likes people who know what they want and ask for what they need.

James 4:3

[3] Ye ask, and receive not, because ye ask amiss, that ye may consume it upon your lusts.

3.3 God can also deliver the poor

There are some people who are poor, and they believe that God will not hear them. However, that is not true, since God listens to every person. Therefore, the poor can pray and God will listen and help them.

Psalm 34:4, 6

[4] I sought the LORD, and he heard me, and delivered me from all my fears.

[6] This poor man cried, and the LORD heard him, and saved him out of all his troubles.

3.4 The Creator will provide for his children

God always wants to provide for his children. He does not want them to live on the crumbs of others, but to seek him and be blessed.

Psalm 34:10

10 The young lions do lack, and suffer hunger: but they that seek the LORD shall not want any good thing.

Mark 11:24

24 Therefore I say unto you, What things soever ye desire, when ye pray, believe that ye receive them, and ye shall have them.

3.5 Be confident in your prayer

When believers pray, they must be confident that God will hear and answer them. While there is always a distraction, they must keep their eyes and minds in great expectation that God will cause them to prosper.

John 15:7, 16

7 If ye abide in me, and my words abide in you, ye shall ask what ye will, and it shall be done unto you.

16 Ye have not chosen me, but I have chosen you, and ordained you, that ye should go and bring forth fruit, and that your fruit should remain: that whatsoever ye shall ask of the Father in my name, he may give it you.

3.6 God's prosperity was evident in Joseph's life

Some persons believe that when God blesses them, he does not want the devil or their enemies to see his blessings upon their lives. However, God likes to boast about the prosperity of his children.

Also, it must be known that God can bless believers wherever they are. While some believers are working for persons who may not appreciate them, they must put their trust in God to bless them. Joseph was blessed while he was working for Pharaoh, and the blessing of God was evident to his master.

Genesis 39:2-5

[2] And the LORD was with Joseph, and he was a prosperous man; and he was in the house of his master the Egyptian. [3] And his master saw that the LORD was with him, and that the LORD made all that he did to prosper in his hand. [4] And Joseph found grace in his sight, and he served him: and he made him overseer over his house, and all that he had he put into his hand. [5] And it came to pass from the time that he had made him overseer in his house, and over all that he had, that the LORD blessed the Egyptian's house for Joseph's sake; and the blessing of the LORD was upon all that he had in the house, and in the field.

When believers are working for various leaders, they must keep their eyes on God for their blessings. It is possible for God to bless them through their leaders. However, believer must never see their leader as their source of blessing, but know that God is their source, and that God chooses to use their leader as a conduit to bless them.

4. Everyone must pray

Too often, some people believe that only some persons must pray. They may think that only leaders must pray, or that only adults must pray.

However, it must be noted that God wants everyone to pray. When more persons pray, God is delighted that more persons understand that he is the answer to all of man's problems and requests. While some things may look simple, people still need to pray about them.

When Jesus said that men ought always to pray, he was not referring only to the male gender, but to everyone. Therefore, he sets the stage for everyone to know that they have a responsibility to seek him. He didn't discriminate against any age or gender, but welcomed everyone to pray. He knew the importance of prayer and did not want to leave anyone out of this wonderful experience.

Luke 18:1

[1] And he spake a parable unto them to this end, that men ought always to pray, and not to faint.

4.1 Men praying

Men must never be ashamed when they have to pray. They must not avoid the opportunity to pray by requesting that women pray on their behalf. God wants men to pray and expects that more of them will pray.

In Job 1:1-5, his sons went to a feast. Being the upright man that he was, Job prayed for his sons. He did not leave anything to chance. Some men would have stayed up and had fun until their sons returned home, but Job used the time to pray. Job did not ask his wife to pray, but he prayed for his sons.

Every parent has the responsibility to pray constantly for their children. No parent can be everywhere with their children at all times, but with their prayer, God will be with their children everywhere.

Job 1:1-5

¹ There was a man in the land of Uz, whose name was Job; and that man was perfect and upright, and one that feared God, and eschewed evil. ² And there were born unto him seven sons and three daughters. ³ His substance also was seven thousand sheep, and three thousand camels, and five hundred yoke of oxen, and five hundred she asses, and a very great household; so that this man was the greatest of all the men of the east. ⁴ And his sons went and feasted in their houses, every one his day; and sent and called for their three sisters to eat and to drink with them. ⁵ And it was so, when the days of their feasting were gone about, that Job sent and sanctified them, and rose early in the morning, and offered burnt offerings according to the number of them all: for Job said, It may be that my sons have sinned, and cursed God in their hearts. Thus did Job continually.

Elijah was another man who was not afraid to pray. He prayed that it would not rain for some years. He had a relationship with God, and God answered his prayer.

1 Kings 17:1

¹ And Elijah the Tishbite, who was of the inhabitants of Gilead, said unto Ahab, As the LORD God of Israel liveth, before whom I stand, there shall not be dew nor rain these years, but according to my word.

If God answered Elijah's prayer, then he will answer the prayers of other men. Therefore, men need to make their prayers known unto God. What men need to know is that God is listening for more men to reach him through prayer. They must take their eyes off of their problems and come boldly before his throne in prayer.

4.1.1 King Jehoshaphat prayed unto God

Jehoshaphat the king was troubled that his enemy was causing his people much discomfort. He chose to seek God, and God did provide him with a word. First of all, God strengthened their spirit, since they were only seeing defeat ahead of them. As God strengthened the king's spirit, the king also encouraged the people to be confident that God would destroy their enemies, according to 2 Chronicles 20:20.

God wants all men to pray. God even said to Jehoshaphat and his men that they need not fight, since God was going to fight the battle for them and destroy the enemy, according to 2 Chronicles 20:15-17. In today's society, too many men are trying to fight battles that they do not have the armory and wisdom to deal with. However, if they take an example from King Jehoshaphat, they will utilize less energy and have more victories.

2 Chronicles 20:1-34

[1] It came to pass after this also, that the children of Moab, and the children of Ammon, and with them other beside the Ammonites, came against Jehoshaphat to battle. [2] Then there came some that told Jehoshaphat, saying, There cometh a great multitude against thee from beyond the sea on this side Syria; and, behold, they be in Hazazontamar, which is Engedi. [3] And Jehoshaphat feared, and set himself to seek the LORD, and proclaimed a fast throughout all Judah. [4] And Judah gathered themselves together, to ask help of the LORD: even out of all the cities of Judah they came to seek the LORD.

[5] And Jehoshaphat stood in the congregation of Judah and Jerusalem, in the house of the LORD, before the new court, [6] And said, O LORD God of our fathers, art not thou God in heaven? and rulest not thou over all the kingdoms of the heathen? and in thine hand is there not power and might, so that none can withstand thee? [7] Art not thou our God, who didst drive out the inhabitants of this land before thy people Israel, and gavest it to the seed of Abraham thy friend for ever? [8] And they dwelt therein, and have built thee a sanctuary therein for thy name, saying, [9] If, when evil cometh upon us, as the sword, judgment, or pestilence, or famine, we stand before this house, and in thy presence, (for thy name is in this house,) and cry unto thee in our affliction, then thou wilt hear and help.

[10] And now, behold, the children of Ammon and Moab and mount Seir, whom thou wouldest not let Israel invade when they came out of the land of Egypt, but they turned from them, and destroyed them not; [11] Behold, I say, how they reward us, to come to cast us out of thy

possession, which thou hast given us to inherit. ¹² O our God, wilt thou not judge them? for we have no might against this great company that cometh against us; neither know we what to do: but our eyes are upon thee.

¹³ And all Judah stood before the LORD, with their little ones, their wives, and their children. ¹⁴ Then upon Jahaziel the son of Zechariah, the son of Benaiah, the son of Jeiel, the son of Mattaniah, a Levite of the sons of Asaph, came the Spirit of the LORD in the midst of the congregation; ¹⁵ And he said, Hearken ye, all Judah, and ye inhabitants of Jerusalem, and thou king Jehoshaphat, Thus saith the LORD unto you, Be not afraid nor dismayed by reason of this great multitude; for the battle is not yours, but God's. ¹⁶ To morrow go ye down against them: behold, they come up by the cliff of Ziz; and ye shall find them at the end of the brook, before the wilderness of Jeruel. ¹⁷ Ye shall not need to fight in this battle: set yourselves, stand ye still, and see the salvation of the LORD with you, O Judah and Jerusalem: fear not, nor be dismayed; to morrow go out against them: for the LORD will be with you.

¹⁸ And Jehoshaphat bowed his head with his face to the ground: and all Judah and the inhabitants of Jerusalem fell before the LORD, worshipping the LORD. ¹⁹ And the Levites, of the children of the Kohathites, and of the children of the Korhites, stood up to praise the LORD God of Israel with a loud voice on high. ²⁰ And they rose early in the morning, and went forth into the wilderness of Tekoa: and as they went forth, Jehoshaphat stood and said, Hear me, O Judah, and ye inhabitants of Jerusalem; Believe in the LORD your God, so shall ye be established; believe his prophets, so shall ye prosper.

²¹ And when he had consulted with the people, he appointed singers unto the LORD, and that should praise the beauty of holiness, as they went out before the army, and to say, Praise the LORD; for his mercy endureth forever. ²² And when they began to sing and to praise, the LORD set ambushments against the children of Ammon, Moab, and mount Seir, which were come against Judah; and they were smitten. ²³ For the children of Ammon and Moab stood up against the inhabitants of mount Seir, utterly to slay and destroy them: and when they had made an end of the inhabitants of Seir, every one helped to destroy another.

24 And when Judah came toward the watch tower in the wilderness, they looked unto the multitude, and, behold, they were dead bodies fallen to the earth, and none escaped. 25 And when Jehoshaphat and his people came to take away the spoil of them, they found among them in abundance both riches with the dead bodies, and precious jewels, which they stripped off for themselves, more than they could carry away: and they were three days in gathering of the spoil, it was so much. 26 And on the fourth day they assembled themselves in the valley of Berachah; for there they blessed the LORD: therefore the name of the same place was called, The valley of Berachah, unto this day.

27 Then they returned, every man of Judah and Jerusalem, and Jehoshaphat in the forefront of them, to go again to Jerusalem with joy; for the LORD had made them to rejoice over their enemies. 28 And they came to Jerusalem with psalteries and harps and trumpets unto the house of the LORD. 29 And the fear of God was on all the kingdoms of those countries, when they had heard that the LORD fought against the enemies of Israel. 30 So the realm of Jehoshaphat was quiet: for his God gave him rest round about.

31 And Jehoshaphat reigned over Judah: he was thirty and five years old when he began to reign, and he reigned twenty and five years in Jerusalem. And his mother's name was Azubah the daughter of Shilhi. 32 And he walked in the way of Asa his father, and departed not from it, doing that which was right in the sight of the LORD. 33 Howbeit the high places were not taken away: for as yet the people had not prepared their hearts unto the God of their fathers. 34 Now the rest of the acts of Jehoshaphat, first and last, behold, they are written in the book of Jehu the son of Hanani, who is mentioned in the book of the kings of Israel.

Take note that after they won the battle, they praised God. When men place God first and God comes through for them, then they must be willing to praise him. For all those who want to be successful, it is important to always keep God in the equation. Some of the battles that men are unable to win with their hands, they will win those battles when God leads them, as they seek God in prayer.

4.1.2 Paul and Silas prayed while in prison

The apostles were in prison. They were there not because they disobeyed God, but because they were doing the work of the Lord, which was contrary to what some people wanted to see. Even when the apostles Paul and Silas were thrown into prison, they did not refuse to pray, but sang songs and prayed.

The scripture bears witness that when they prayed and sang songs, God heard them. Not only did God hear them, but he also opened the prison and caused them to walk out of the prison as free men. That is how important prayer is: when men seek God, their problems will vanish.

Acts 16:23-33

23 And when they had laid many stripes upon them, they cast them into prison, charging the jailor to keep them safely: 24 Who, having received such a charge, thrust them into the inner prison, and made their feet fast in the stocks. 25 And at midnight Paul and Silas prayed, and sang praises unto God: and the prisoners heard them. 26 And suddenly there was a great earthquake, so that the foundations of the prison were shaken: and immediately all the doors were opened, and every one's bands were loosed. 27 And the keeper of the prison awaking out of his sleep, and seeing the prison doors open, he drew out his sword, and would have killed himself, supposing that the prisoners had been fled. 28 But Paul cried with a loud voice, saying, Do thyself no harm: for we are all here. 29 Then he called for a light, and sprang in, and came trembling, and fell down before Paul and Silas, 30 And brought them out, and said, Sirs, what must I do to be saved? 31 And they said, Believe on the Lord Jesus Christ, and thou shalt be saved, and thy house. 32 And they spake unto him the word of the Lord, and to all that were in his house. 33 And he took them the same hour of the night, and washed their stripes; and was baptized, he and all his, straightway.

God is willing to save people when his children seek him. The action God took to deliver Paul and Silas caused the keeper of the prison to seek the same God whom Paul and Silas served (Acts 16:31).

4.2 Women praying

While men must pray, women must also pray, as their prayers are also important to God. The Lord is looking for many women to come before him in prayer.

In the book of Esther, particularly in the fourth chapter, we read that her people were in trouble. It was not lawful for her to see the king, but she was willing to make a sacrifice. She knew that prayer was important, so she did just that. As a result of her seeking God in prayer, she was given access to the king, and the king was willing to grant her request. If she had gone in her own strength, she would have failed, and the children of God would have remained in bondage or even been killed.

Therefore, women must not be afraid to pray, and they must make their petition known unto God. It is known that God will listen to everyone's prayer and reward them in due season. It is time now to see what happened with Esther, her prayer, and the results.

Esther 4:1-17

1 When Mordecai perceived all that was done, Mordecai rent his clothes, and put on sackcloth with ashes, and went out into the midst of the city, and cried with a loud and a bitter cry; 2 And came even before the king's gate: for none might enter into the king's gate clothed with sackcloth. 3 And in every province, whithersoever the king's commandment and his decree came, there was great mourning among the Jews, and fasting, and weeping, and wailing; and many lay in sackcloth and ashes. 4 So Esther's maids and her chamberlains came and told it her. Then was the queen exceedingly grieved; and she sent raiment to clothe Mordecai, and to take away his sackcloth from him: but he received it not. 5 Then called Esther for Hatach, one of the king's chamberlains, whom he had appointed to attend upon her, and gave him a commandment to Mordecai, to know what it was, and why it was.

6 So Hatach went forth to Mordecai unto the street of the city, which was before the king's gate. 7 And Mordecai told him of all that had happened unto him, and of the sum of the money that Haman had promised to pay to the king's treasuries for the Jews, to destroy them. 8 Also he gave him the copy of the writing of the decree that was given at Shushan to destroy them, to shew it unto Esther, and to

declare it unto her, and to charge her that she should go in unto the king, to make supplication unto him, and to make request before him for her people. [9] And Hatach came and told Esther the words of Mordecai.

[10] Again Esther spake unto Hatach, and gave him commandment unto Mordecai; [11] All the king's servants, and the people of the king's provinces, do know, that whosoever, whether man or women, shall come unto the king into the inner court, who is not called, there is one law of his to put him to death, except such to whom the king shall hold out the golden sceptre, that he may live: but I have not been called to come in unto the king these thirty days. [12] And they told to Mordecai Esther's words.

[13] Then Mordecai commanded to answer Esther, Think not with thyself that thou shalt escape in the king's house, more than all the Jews. [14] For if thou altogether holdest thy peace at this time, then shall there enlargement and deliverance arise to the Jews from another place; but thou and thy father's house shall be destroyed: and who knoweth whether thou art come to the kingdom for such a time as this? [15] Then Esther bade them return Mordecai this answer, [16] Go, gather together all the Jews that are present in Shushan, and fast ye for me, and neither eat nor drink three days, night or day: I also and my maidens will fast likewise; and so will I go in unto the king, which is not according to the law: and if I perish, I perish. [17] So Mordecai went his way, and did according to all that Esther had commanded him.

Esther did not pray alone; she involved others in praying. Her actions were made more impactful as other like-minded persons were praying for the same thing. Esther only went to the king after she prayed and fasted. Believers must do a similar thing. They must not go in their own strength, but allow God to go before them.

When God goes before his people, he will perform miracles. While it was against the law for Esther to approach the king without an invitation, she was willing to put her life at risk. She did not want to see God's people suffer, and she was willing to die if that was the alternative.

Esther's concern was for the people of God to be delivered, and God honored her prayer. God's people must know that when they put him first, he will be their deliverer.

4.3 Children praying

Children are important in God's sight, and he wants them to pray. God listens to the voice of his children as they seek him, so parents need to encourage their children to pray.

Some adults want to think that because children may not be mature in their thinking, they may not have the right set of words to use when they are praying. God doesn't respond to children based upon their choice of words when they pray, but based upon their heart.

5. Teach us to pray

When the disciples were with Jesus, they saw him do many great things before their eyes. They liked what they saw and thought that they could do the same things. Many of the things that God wants his children to do require prayer.

Since Jesus knew that prayer is important, he taught his disciples to pray. Many persons may believe that the disciples should already have known to pray. However, when they listened to the prayer that Jesus taught them, it was different from any other prayer that they had ever heard.

The prayer that Jesus shared with them included forgiveness. This may be a strange thing for some believers, as they do not believe that they have to forgive persons. However, those who want God to operate on their behalf must be willing to forgive others and even themselves.

Matthew 6:6-15

6 But thou, when thou prayest, enter into thy closet, and when thou hast shut thy door, pray to thy Father which is in secret; and thy Father which seeth in secret shall reward thee openly. 7 But when ye pray, use not vain repetitions, as the heathen do: for they think that they shall be heard for their much speaking. 8 Be not ye, therefore, like unto them: for your Father knoweth what things ye have need of, before ye ask him.

9 After this manner, therefore, pray ye: Our Father which art in heaven, Hallowed be thy name. 10 Thy kingdom come, Thy will be done in earth, as it is in heaven. 11 Give us this day our daily bread. 12 And forgive us our debts, as we forgive our debtors. 13 And lead us not into temptation, but deliver us from evil: For thine is the kingdom, and the power, and the glory, forever. Amen. 14 For if ye forgive men their trespasses, your heavenly Father will also forgive you: 15 But if ye

forgive not men their trespasses, neither will your Father forgive your trespasses.

God knows every believer's needs, yet he asks them to pray. Jesus told the disciples that when you pray, you should enter your closet. There is an important lesson to be learned by every believer according to Matthew 6:6-8. While God is listening to those loud and public prayers, he wants every believer to find a private place and pray. When they are in a private place, they must seek God and also seek to forgive people of their sins.

Those believers who want to have an impactful prayer life must allow the Lord to teach them to pray. Prayer is simple but must include some important things. This includes, but is not limited to, placing God ahead of every situation. Those who acknowledge that only God will answer their prayer can rest assured that he will work on their behalf.

The needs of people will be provided by God. Therefore, they must ask God daily to give them their daily bread. Another thing to note in this passage of scripture is that believers need to seek God daily. Therefore, even if they received their breakthrough yesterday, they must go before God today for him to bless them.

Temptation is all around us. It appears that these days, people do not have to go and look for temptation; the temptation is constantly coming to them. However, they must ask God not to lead them into temptation but to lead them away from it.

6. Nothing happens until you pray

Every believer must know that nothing happens unless they pray. Some believers may not want to accept this fact, but God wants everyone to call on him.

To show the three stages of prayer, the word **ASK** will be broken down into its three separate letters. Each letter will be explained, and it will show the different levels of intensity of praying unto God.

The scripture reference for this explanation is Matthew 7:7-8.

Matthew 7:7-8

[7] Ask, and it shall be given you; seek, and ye shall find; knock, and it shall be opened unto you: [8] For every one that asketh receiveth; and he that seeketh findeth; and to him that knocketh it shall be opened.

Figure 11. Intensify your effort to seek God for your blessing (Matthew 7:7-8)

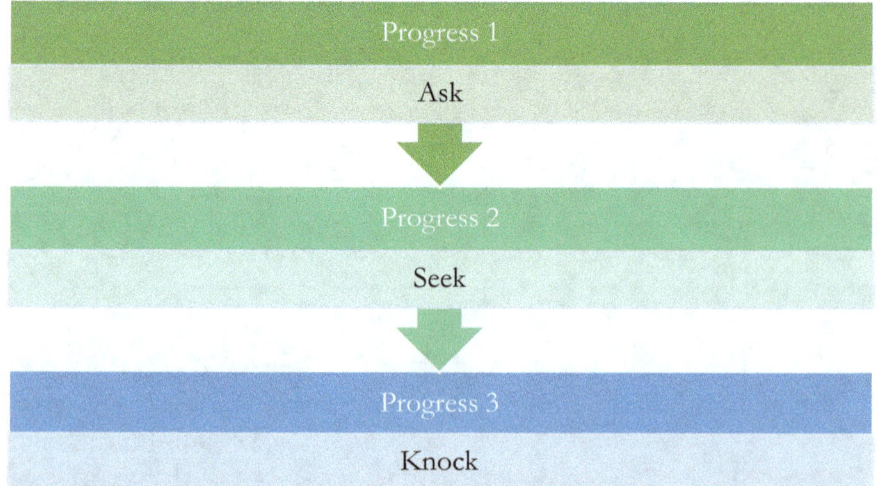

6.1 Letter "A"

With the letter A, persons will make their request known unto the Lord. Many persons often do this, but some leave the altar without showing any intensity. While God wants to do many things for his children, he sometimes looks to see how desperate his children are, and sad to say, many times, believers just place their prayer before God and walk away.

6.2 Letter "S"

Beyond placing a prayer before God, believers must seek more of God during their time of prayer. Most times, believers want something from God, but they are not willing to seek more of God through prayer.

If believers draw near to God, they will see more evidence of his work on their behalf. Every believer must move beyond asking to seeking. Those who seek God must know that they will not lack anything. God so loves to bless us that the psalmist wrote in Psalm 37:25, "I have been young, and now am old; yet have I not seen the righteous forsaken, nor his seed begging bread". When we make prayer our lifestyle instead of just an occasional thing, God will even provide for our future generations.

Psalm 34:10

10 The young lions do lack, and suffer hunger: but they that seek the LORD shall not want any good thing.

Jesus provided a story to the listeners, talking about a woman who had ten pieces of silver. He mentioned that one of the pieces of silver was lost, and this woman sought until she found that silver piece. Every believer must cherish that which God has given or promised them. Therefore, they must constantly seek God until all of the promises are fulfilled in their lives.

Luke 15:8-9

8 Either what woman having ten pieces of silver, if she lose one piece, doth not light a candle, and sweep the house, and seek diligently till she find it? 9 And when she hath found it, she calleth her friends and her neighbours together, saying, Rejoice with me; for I have found the piece which I had lost.

6.3 Letter "K"

This last letter, "K," speaks to the level of intensity where a believer keeps knocking at the door, or the strength that they utilize to knock at the door has increased. At this stage, believers are almost saying, "God, I will not leave you until you bless me." This shows that believers are not willing to return to their place of discomfort or comfort, but they need an answer from God, and they need that answer immediately.

If believers are willing to get to this stage, they will have more victories. At this stage, the letter "K" is likened to a believer who will kick down the door to enter God's presence and demand their blessings. In a literal sense, of course, no one can kick down a door that God has, but it implies that they are so desperate that they refuse to return home empty-handed.

Too many believers are quick to walk away without their victory. It is always God's intention to bless his children, but do his children want to be blessed by him?

It is important to read this story about Jacob wrestling with the angel. In this scripture, one sees that Jacob was not willing to allow the angel to leave until he was blessed. This must be the approach taken by all believers.

Genesis 32:24-32

24 And Jacob was left alone, and there wrestled a man with him until the breaking of the day. 25 And when he saw that he prevailed not against him, he touched the hollow of his thigh; and the hollow of Jacob's thigh was out of joint, as he wrestled with him. 26 And he said, Let me go, for the day breaketh. And he said, I will not let thee go, except thou bless me. 27 And he said unto him, What is thy name? And he said, Jacob. 28 And he said, Thy name shall be called no more Jacob, but Israel: for as a prince hast thou power with God and with men, and hast prevailed.

29 And Jacob asked him, and said, Tell me, I pray thee, thy name. And he said, Wherefore is it that thou dost ask after my name? And he blessed him there. 30 And Jacob called the name of the place Peniel: for I have seen God face to face, and my life is preserved. 31 And as he passed over Penuel the sun rose upon him, and he halted upon his thigh. 32 Therefore the children of Israel eat not of the sinew which shrank, which is upon the hollow of the thigh, unto this day: because he touched the hollow of Jacob's thigh in the sinew that shrank.

Some Bible references state that Jacob wrestled with God, while others say that he wrestled with an angel, and others say that he wrestled with a man. For simplicity's sake in this example, it will be assumed that he wrestled with an angel.

Figure 12. What happened when Jacob wrestled with the angel?

While this passage of scripture in Genesis 32:24-32 may appear to be an ordinary story, it reveals many things that will occur when a person knocks at God's door until something happens. If believers take an example from Jacob's life in this passage of scripture, they will know that they must not be willing to give up easily. Jacob's thigh was disjointed, but he never gave up wrestling with the angel. He knew that he was in pain, but the pain made him wrestle more with the angel until he was blessed.

Can believers wrestle during their time of pain until they get their breakthrough? It is hopeful that they will now move beyond asking and seeking to knock until they get their breakthrough.

7. Prayer moves mountains

There will always be mountains in the path of every believer. If a believer has not experienced any mountain since they have been serving the Lord, then they need to reexamine their life.

Sometimes, God sees the devil placing obstacles in front of believers' paths, and he is watching to see what their response will be. It is not that God hates or neglect his children, but he knows that he has taught them enough about how to survive through him.

Natural mountains are made of sedimentary materials. Most persons can go to such a mountain and touch it. Some mountains are very beautiful, so persons will visit them and take photographs, or climb them as part of an expedition.

However, not all mountains are natural. In a believer's life, they will be faced with mountains, mainly in two major categories: physical and spiritual. Take note that physical mountains are not just made with sedimentary materials, but they can be seen and touched. Spiritual mountains have no shape and are impossible for persons to see and touch. Therefore, every believer must have spiritual eyes to see spiritual mountains.

Table 1. Mountains in front of believers

Physical mountains	Spiritual mountains
Friends	Fear
Family	Poverty
Workmates	Ill health
Neighbors	Lack of vision
Companions	Demons

7.1 Believers are called to wrestle against principalities

Every believer who wants to accomplish much in God must be willing to wrestle against Satan's devices. The battle is often an intense one, but with God, believers will overcome.

Ephesians 6:10-18

[10] Finally, my brethren, be strong in the Lord, and in the power of his might. [11] Put on the whole armour of God, that ye may be able to stand against the wiles of the devil. [12] For we wrestle not against flesh and blood, but against principalities, against powers, against the rulers of the darkness of this world, against spiritual wickedness in high places. [13] Wherefore take unto you the whole armour of God, that ye may be able to withstand in the evil day and having done all, to stand. [14] Stand therefore, having your loins girt about with truth, and having on the breastplate of righteousness; [15] And your feet shod with the preparation of the gospel of peace; [16] Above all, taking the shield of faith, wherewith ye shall be able to quench all the fiery darts of the wicked. [17] And take the helmet of salvation, and the sword of the Spirit, which is the word of God: [18] Praying always with all prayer and supplication in the Spirit, and watching thereunto with all perseverance and supplication for all saints.

Believers are constantly having battles with the adversary. Sometimes, before one battle is completed, another battle starts. Satan plans to constantly place obstacles in front of every believer.

When Jesus walked on this earth, he operated as a human. Matthew 21:18 tells us about a time when he was hungry. He expected the fig tree to be productive at that time, but there were no figs on the tree at the time of his visit. Jesus had performed other miracles, and the disciples marveled at what he had done. He cursed the fig tree and the tree withered. Take note, Jesus could have blessed the fig tree, but he chose to curse it instead.

Believers must learn from this story that they have the power to speak life and death. Also, with the power that believers have, they can speak to anything and there can be instant results, but they need to have faith in their prayer, and their relationship must be constant with the Lord.

Matthew 21:18-21

[18] Now in the morning as he returned into the city, he hungered. [19] And when he saw a fig tree in the way, he came to it, and found nothing thereon, but leaves only, and said unto it, Let no fruit grow on thee henceforward forever. And presently the fig tree withered away. [20] And when the disciples saw it, they marvelled, saying, How soon is the fig tree withered away! [21] Jesus answered and said unto them, Verily I say unto you, If ye have faith, and doubt not, ye shall not only do this which is done to the fig tree, but also if ye shall say unto this mountain, Be thou removed, and be thou cast into the sea; it shall be done.

While many mountains stand in front of believers, each believer just needs to speak to those mountains. The mountains may look large, but with prayer, they will become a valley. Prayer is a great resource, and every believer must use that resource wisely so that they will walk in victory.

Figure 13. Jesus' actions and the fig tree's response

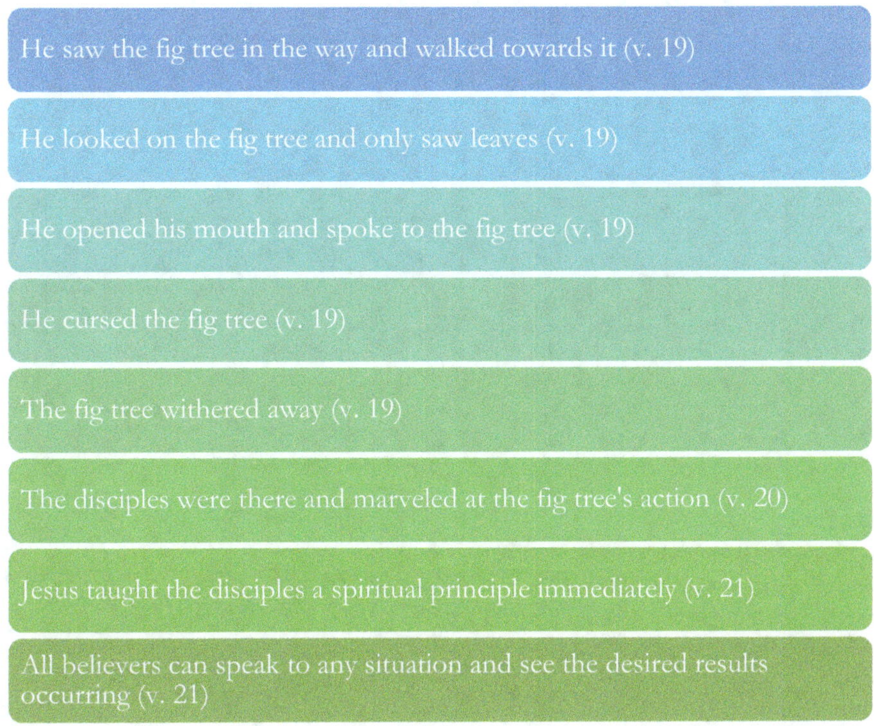

Jesus was quick to draw a parallel and let the disciples know that they can speak to any situation and see their prayer become a reality. It must be noted that Jesus could have walked away from the fig tree, but he had an important lesson to share with his disciples. When they saw what he did, they marveled.

As believers speak and work for the Lord, they are doing so with God's authority. Therefore, believers are not powerless, but powerful.

1 Peter 4:11

[11] If any man speaks, let him speak as the oracles of God; if any man minister, let him do it as of the ability which God giveth: that God in all things may be glorified through Jesus Christ, to whom be praise and dominion for ever and ever. Amen.

8. Prayer opens the prison door

There are believers locked in different kinds of prisons, and each kind can affect their very lives.

Figure 14. Prisons that affect a believer's life

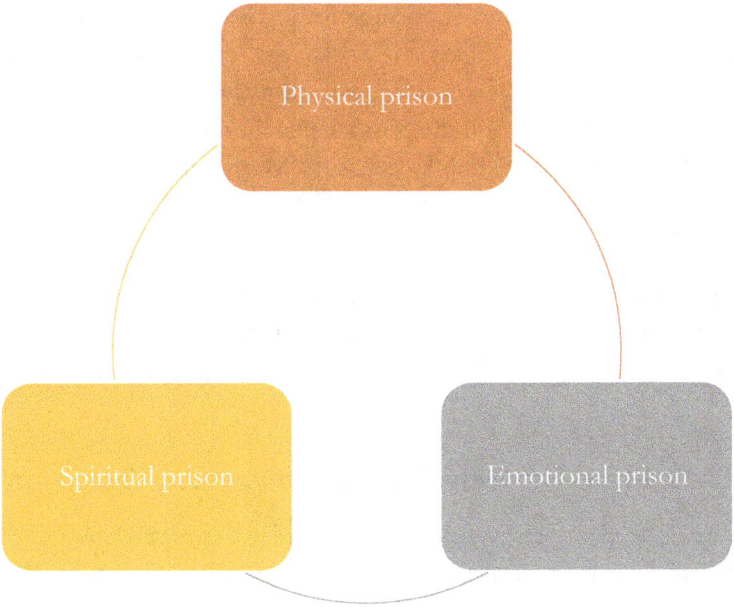

8.1 Physical prison

When a person violates the law, they are often taken before a court. Once the judge or magistrate pronounces that they are guilty and they have to be sentenced, then they are placed into a physical prison.

This type of prison places many restrictions on a person's physical movement. They are unable to see their family and friends. There have restricted visiting hours. The food provided to the prisoners is often prepared by the prison authorities, unless their relatives choose to provide food for the prisoner.

8.2 Emotional prison

Unlike a physical prison, with an emotional prison, persons are often trapped in their thinking and behaviors. In many relationships, persons find themselves trapped and unable to think for themselves. In this kind of relationship, one member of the family will place restrictions on the other; despite knowing that some things are wrong, they will comply with their compelling partner or parent.

Even in places of employment, some employers have established emotional prisons for their employees. These employees are restricted in their attitudes and actions because their superior is a boss rather than a leader.

Those who operate as a boss make the employees feel worthless. Employees only work with those organizations because they want to earn, but are often dissatisfied with the boss's behaviour. More organizations need leaders who care about the employees and allow them to be creative.

8.3 Spiritual prison

Satan wants all believers to find themselves in a spiritual prison. He does not want them to see the benefits and blessings that God has in store for them. He often tries to blind their eyes to that which the Lord wants them to have.

8.4 God can destroy physical prisons for his children's sake

Every believer must be optimistic that if they are wrongly placed into prison, God can deliver them.

Acts 16:23-33

23 And when they had laid many stripes upon them, they cast them into prison, charging the jailor to keep them safely: 24 Who, having received such a charge, thrust them into the inner prison, and made their feet fast in the stocks. 25 And at midnight Paul and Silas prayed, and sang praises unto God: and the prisoners heard them. 26 And suddenly there was a great earthquake so that the foundations of the prison were

shaken: and immediately all the doors were opened, and every one's bands were loosed. ²⁷ And the keeper of the prison awaking out of his sleep, and seeing the prison doors open, he drew out his sword, and would have killed himself, supposing that the prisoners had been fled. ²⁸ But Paul cried with a loud voice, saying, Do thyself no harm: for we are all here. ²⁹ Then he called for a light, and sprang in, and came trembling, and fell down before Paul and Silas, ³⁰ And brought them out, and said, Sirs, what must I do to be saved? ³¹ And they said, Believe on the Lord Jesus Christ, and thou shalt be saved, and thy house. ³² And they spake unto him the word of the Lord, and to all that were in his house. ³³ And he took them the same hour of the night, and washed their stripes; and was baptized, he and all his, straightway.

From the passage above, it is clear that Paul and Silas were thrown into prison for doing the work of the Lord. This prison was physical. However, as they prayed and sang songs (Acts 16:25-26), God heard them and destroyed the physical prison. Just imagine, if God can destroy a physical prison, then he can also destroy other things for his children's sake.

Paul and Silas were saved when God destroyed the physical prison, and God also causes many other persons to be saved. Prayer is powerful, and every believer must pray unto God, no matter their situation.

8.5 God destroys emotional prisons for his children's sake

God wants every believer to be free emotionally. To find this emotional freedom, they have to renew their minds. They have to let the same mind that was in Christ be also in them. When the mind is free, people can walk away from bondage.

Romans 12:1-2

¹ I beseech you therefore, brethren, by the mercies of God, that ye present your bodies a living sacrifice, holy, acceptable unto God, which is your reasonable service. ² And be not conformed to this world: but be ye transformed by the renewing of your mind, that ye may prove what is that good, and acceptable, and perfect, will of God.

The apostle Paul admonishes the believers to keep their thinking in Christ. They are not to exalt themselves. He goes on to say in 2 Corinthians 10:4 that the believer's warfare is not carnal. Therefore, they must be involved in an emotional and spiritual battle and not a physical one.

2 Corinthians 10:1-6

[1] Now I Paul myself beseech you by the meekness and gentleness of Christ, who in presence am base among you, but being absent am bold toward you: [2] But I beseech you, that I may not be bold when I am present with that confidence, wherewith I think to be bold against some, which think of us as if we walked according to the flesh. [3] For though we walk in the flesh, we do not war after the flesh: [4] (For the weapons of our warfare are not carnal, but mighty through God to the pulling down of strong holds;) [5] Casting down imaginations, and every high thing that exalteth itself against the knowledge of God, and bringing into captivity every thought to the obedience of Christ; [6] And having in a readiness to revenge all disobedience, when your obedience is fulfilled.

8.6 God destroys the spiritual prison for his children's sake

Many persons are still trapped in a spiritual prison and wondering if they can come out of it. Therefore, the gospel has to be preached to everyone. Those who are locked in spiritual prison will only be delivered through the word of God and by his Spirit.

For every believer whose family members are locked in a spiritual prison, they need to pray for their loved ones and friends.

Galatians 5:16-24

[16] This I say then, Walk in the Spirit, and ye shall not fulfil the lust of the flesh. [17] For the flesh lusteth against the Spirit, and the Spirit against the flesh: and these are contrary the one to the other: so that ye cannot do the things that ye would. [18] But if ye be led of the Spirit, ye are not under the law. [19] Now the works of the flesh are manifest, which are these; Adultery, fornication, uncleanness, lasciviousness, [20] Idolatry, witchcraft, hatred, variance, emulations, wrath, strife, seditions, heresies, [21] Envyings, murders, drunkenness, revellings, and such like: of the which I tell you before, as I have also told you in time past, that they which do such things shall not inherit the kingdom of God. [22] But the fruit of the Spirit is love, joy, peace, longsuffering,

gentleness, goodness, faith, 23 Meekness, temperance: against such there is no law. 24 And they that are Christ's have crucified the flesh with the affections and lusts.

The apostle Paul tells all persons to walk after the Spirit and not the flesh. Many persons have placed themselves in prison because they are walking after the flesh.

Jesus was quick to point out that if anyone is in bondage, the Son can set them free. This freedom is not from a physical prison, but a spiritual prison, which will cause them to die and go to hell if they are not freed from it. Christ is so kind that he wants everyone to be saved and he extends his loving arms to everyone. Those whom he has set free are free indeed.

John 8:31-36

31 Then said Jesus to those Jews which believed on him, If ye continue in my word, then are ye my disciples indeed; 32 And ye shall know the truth, and the truth shall make you free. 33 They answered him, We be Abraham's seed, and were never in bondage to any man: how sayest thou, Ye shall be made free? 34 Jesus answered them, Verily, verily, I say unto you, Whosoever committeth sin is the servant of sin. 35 And the servant abideth not in the house for ever: but the Son abideth ever. 36 If the Son therefore shall make you free, ye shall be free indeed.

Believers must pray for persons to be set free. Many persons need deliverance, but someone ought to pray for them.

All believers must equip themselves with the things that make them effective for spiritual battles. The apostle Paul provides all believers with tools that they must use to fight in every spiritual battle, which are not the same as those used for a physical battle.

Ephesians 6:10-18

10 Finally, my brethren, be strong in the Lord, and in the power of his might. 11 Put on the whole armour of God, that ye may be able to stand against the wiles of the devil. 12 For we wrestle not against flesh and blood, but against principalities, against powers, against the rulers of the darkness of this world, against spiritual wickedness in high places. 13 Wherefore take unto you the whole armour of God, that ye may be able to withstand in the evil day and having done all, to stand. 14 Stand

therefore, having your loins girt about with truth, and having on the breastplate of righteousness; [15] And your feet shod with the preparation of the gospel of peace; [16] Above all, taking the shield of faith, wherewith ye shall be able to quench all the fiery darts of the wicked. [17] And take the helmet of salvation, and the sword of the Spirit, which is the word of God: [18] Praying always with all prayer and supplication in the Spirit, and watching thereunto with all perseverance and supplication for all saints.

9. Prayer causes rain to come

One of the things believers can pray for is rain. While rain is a natural event and God has full control over it, he gives his children the power to pray for rain.

1 Kings 17:1

[1] And Elijah the Tishbite, who was of the inhabitants of Gilead, said unto Ahab, As the LORD God of Israel liveth, before whom I stand, there shall not be dew nor rain these years, but according to my word.

1 Kings 18:41-46

[41] And Elijah said unto Ahab, Get thee up, eat and drink; for there is a sound of abundance of rain. [42] So Ahab went up to eat and to drink. And Elijah went up to the top of Carmel; and he cast himself down upon the earth, and put his face between his knees, [43] And said to his servant, Go up now, look toward the sea. And he went up, and looked, and said, There is nothing. And he said, Go again seven times. [44] And it came to pass at the seventh time, that he said, Behold, there ariseth a little cloud out of the sea, like a man's hand. And he said, Go up, say unto Ahab, Prepare thy chariot, and get thee down that the rain stop thee not. [45] And it came to pass in the mean while, that the heaven was black with clouds and wind, and there was a great rain. And Ahab rode, and went to Jezreel. [46] And the hand of the LORD was on Elijah, and he girded up his loins, and ran before Ahab to the entrance of Jezreel.

King Ahab wanted to destroy those who served the Lord. However, he had to contend with the prophet Elijah. Therefore, when King Ahab did all that he wanted to do, Elijah proved to him that the God whom he served is very powerful.

Take note that in 1 Kings 17:1, Elijah showed King Ahab that he could pray to Jehovah to suspend the rain and dew. This was something that neither King Ahab nor his mighty men could do. Elijah also said to them that only when he prayed would the rain come again.

After a long period of drought, Elijah sought God's intervention, and then it rained again. 1 Kings 18:41-46 bears evidence that Elijah went up to Mount Carmel and prayed, and God answered his prayer and caused rain to come again. While Elijah sent his servant to see if there was a cloud, the servant did not see the cloud on the first six occasions. However, on the seventh occasion, the servant saw a little cloud.

When believers pray and do not doubt in their hearts, then God can do anything. While rain is a natural event, when believers pray, God can shut up heaven or open heaven for the rain to come.

Matthew 18:18-19

[18] Verily I say unto you, Whatsoever ye shall bind on earth shall be bound in heaven: and whatsoever ye shall loose on earth shall be loosed in heaven. [19] Again I say unto you, That if two of you shall agree on earth as touching any thing that they shall ask, it shall be done for them of my Father which is in heaven.

Therefore, every believer must be willing to exercise their rights according to the power that God has vested in their lives. Many persons do not have access to natural things, but believers have power over natural and supernatural things through prayer. It is expected that as more believers pray unto the Lord, they will see their prayers being manifested.

10. Prayer causes fire to come down

Some persons consider believers as ordinary persons. However, when believers pray to their God, great things can happen.

The story of Elijah and Ahab draws much attention to the power of God and the power of the adversary. Oftentimes, the adversary believes that he can destroy the children of God, and he looks for occasions to embarrass believers. One of the ways Satan operates is to cause situations where believers will become fearful.

However, those believers who know their God can expect great things to happen. God will do great exploits to protect his children.

Daniel 11:32

32 And such as do wickedly against the covenant shall he corrupt by flatteries: but the people that do know their God shall be strong, and do exploits.

10.1 God will destroy evil with fire

Elijah was put to the test to defend his faith. He was not afraid of the challenge, nor was he afraid of what his God could do. The desire that Elijah had in proving his God must be shared by all believers.

Elijah's life was threatened, which is a tough position for anyone to be in. If he chose to surrender, his life would be taken. While it was not King Ahab who was offended by Elijah, he was willing to carry out the demands of his wife, Jezebel. Elijah became the subject of persecution because his actions were contrary to the king's direction.

1 Kings 18:1-40

1 And it came to pass after many days, that the word of the LORD came to Elijah in the third year, saying, Go, shew thyself unto Ahab; and I

will send rain upon the earth. 2 And Elijah went to shew himself unto Ahab. And there was a sore famine in Samaria. 3 And Ahab called Obadiah, which was the governor of his house. (Now Obadiah feared the LORD greatly: 4 For it was so, when Jezebel cut off the prophets of the LORD, that Obadiah took an hundred prophets, and hid them by fifty in a cave, and fed them with bread and water.) 5 And Ahab said unto Obadiah, Go into the land, unto all fountains of water, and unto all brooks: peradventure we may find grass to save the horses and mules alive, that we lose not all the beasts. 6 So they divided the land between them to pass throughout it: Ahab went one way by himself, and Obadiah went another way by himself.

7 And as Obadiah was in the way, behold, Elijah met him: and he knew him, and fell on his face, and said, Art thou that my lord Elijah? 8 And he answered him, I am: go, tell thy lord, Behold, Elijah is here. 9 And he said, What have I sinned, that thou wouldest deliver thy servant into the hand of Ahab, to slay me? 10 As the LORD thy God liveth, there is no nation or kingdom, whither my lord hath not sent to seek thee: and when they said, He is not there; he took an oath of the kingdom and nation, that they found thee not. 11 And now thou sayest, Go, tell thy lord, Behold, Elijah is here. 12 And it shall come to pass, as soon as I am gone from thee, that the Spirit of the LORD shall carry thee whither I know not; and so when I come and tell Ahab, and he cannot find thee, he shall slay me: but I thy servant fear the LORD from my youth. 13 Was it not told my lord what I did when Jezebel slew the prophets of the LORD, how I hid an hundred men of the LORD's prophets by fifty in a cave, and fed them with bread and water? 14 And now thou sayest, Go, tell thy lord, Behold, Elijah is here: and he shall slay me. 15 And Elijah said, As the LORD of hosts liveth, before whom I stand, I will surely shew myself unto him to day.

16 So Obadiah went to meet Ahab, and told him: and Ahab went to meet Elijah. 17 And it came to pass, when Ahab saw Elijah, that Ahab said unto him, Art thou he that troubleth Israel? 18 And he answered, I have not troubled Israel; but thou, and thy father's house, in that ye have forsaken the commandments of the LORD, and thou hast followed Baalim. 19 Now therefore send, and gather to me all Israel unto mount Carmel, and the prophets of Baal four hundred and fifty,

and the prophets of the groves four hundred, which eat at Jezebel's table.

20 So Ahab sent unto all the children of Israel, and gathered the prophets together unto mount Carmel. 21 And Elijah came unto all the people, and said, How long halt ye between two opinions? if the LORD be God, follow him: but if Baal, then follow him. And the people answered him not a word. 22 Then said Elijah unto the people, I, even I only, remain a prophet of the LORD; but Baal's prophets are four hundred and fifty men. 23 Let them therefore give us two bullocks; and let them choose one bullock for themselves, and cut it in pieces, and lay it on wood, and put no fire under: and I will dress the other bullock, and lay it on wood, and put no fire under: 24 And call ye on the name of your gods, and I will call on the name of the LORD: and the God that answereth by fire, let him be God. And all the people answered and said, It is well spoken. 25 And Elijah said unto the prophets of Baal, Choose you one bullock for yourselves, and dress it first; for ye are many; and call on the name of your gods, but put no fire under.

26 And they took the bullock which was given them, and they dressed it, and called on the name of Baal from morning even until noon, saying, O Baal, hear us. But there was no voice, nor any that answered. And they leaped upon the altar which was made. 27 And it came to pass at noon, that Elijah mocked them, and said, Cry aloud: for he is a god; either he is talking, or he is pursuing, or he is in a journey, or peradventure he sleepeth, and must be awaked. 28 And they cried aloud, and cut themselves after their manner with knives and lancets, till the blood gushed out upon them. 29 And it came to pass, when midday was past, and they prophesied until the time of the offering of the evening sacrifice, that there was neither voice, nor any to answer, nor any that regarded.

30 And Elijah said unto all the people, Come near unto me. And all the people came near unto him. And he repaired the altar of the LORD that was broken down. 31 And Elijah took twelve stones, according to the number of the tribes of the sons of Jacob, unto whom the word of the LORD came, saying, Israel shall be thy name: 32 And with the stones he built an altar in the name of the LORD: and he made a trench about the altar, as great as would contain two measures of seed. 33 And he put the wood in order, and cut the bullock in pieces, and laid him

on the wood, and said, Fill four barrels with water, and pour it on the burnt sacrifice, and on the wood. 34 And he said, Do it the second time. And they did it the second time. And he said, Do it the third time. And they did it the third time. 35 And the water ran round about the altar, and he filled the trench also with water.

36 And it came to pass at the time of the offering of the evening sacrifice, that Elijah the prophet came near, and said, LORD God of Abraham, Isaac, and of Israel, let it be known this day that thou art God in Israel, and that I am thy servant, and that I have done all these things at thy word. 37 Hear me, O LORD, hear me, that this people may know that thou art the LORD God, and that thou hast turned their heart back again. 38 Then the fire of the LORD fell, and consumed the burnt sacrifice, and the wood, and the stones, and the dust, and licked up the water that was in the trench. 39 And when all the people saw it, they fell on their faces: and they said, The LORD, he is the God; the LORD, he is the God. 40 And Elijah said unto them, Take the prophets of Baal; let not one of them escape. And they took them: and Elijah brought them down to the brook Kishon, and slew them there.

The prophet Elijah met King Ahab face to face, and Elijah was not afraid of the challenge of King Ahab. He asked the king to gather all of his prophets, meaning those who served Baal. This was about to be a great showdown. It was Elijah against a large contingent, but God was on Elijah's side. When Elijah prayed and called down fire from heaven, God responded to his request and consumed the sacrifices. That is the power of prayer when believers place God in front of everything that they do. King Ahab and all his mighty men could not respond to the power of God.

The same power that Elijah experienced is still available today. God has never lost his power. As believers pray, God will destroy the works of darkness. When the enemy plans to destroy a believer, and the believer prays, then God will come to their rescue.

This is how God defends his children against the devil when we pray. The Bible says in Isaiah 59:19, "So shall they fear the name of the Lord from the west, and his glory from the rising of the sun. When the enemy shall come in like a flood, the Spirit of the LORD shall lift up a standard against him."

11. Prayer for deliverance

Some persons are affected by sickness and demons. While medical doctors can assist those who are affected by medical issues, they are unable to help persons who are possessed by demons.

People cannot see demons with their physical eyes; they need the help of the Lord to see them in the spirit. No one must simply accept sickness and demon possession. Therefore, those who are possessed will need help.

Many churches offer deliverance services to their members and to the public, in which many persons who have some strange sicknesses will be delivered. Some of these persons visited doctors but did not receive any medical assistance.

Persons who are possessed by demons often operate in strange ways. While a person who is free from demonic possession will operate normally, someone who is possessed will respond differently to the same condition.

Believers are key to the deliverance of those who are possessed. However, not everyone within the church can be involved in the casting out of demons. Look at this example of some men who attempted to cast out demons, but were not empowered by the Lord to do so.

Acts 19:13-20

13 Then certain of the vagabond Jews, exorcists, took upon them to call over them which had evil spirits the name of the LORD Jesus, saying, We adjure you by Jesus whom Paul preacheth. 14 And there were seven sons of one Sceva, a Jew, and chief of the priests, which did so. 15 And the evil spirit answered and said, Jesus I know, and Paul I know; but who are ye? 16 And the man in whom the evil spirit was leaped on them, and overcame them, and prevailed against them, so that they fled out of that house naked and wounded. 17 And this was known to all the Jews and Greeks also dwelling at Ephesus, and fear

fell on them all, and the name of the Lord Jesus was magnified. [18] And many that believed came, and confessed, and shewed their deeds. [19] Many of them also which used curious arts brought their books together, and burned them before all men: and they counted the price of them, and found it fifty thousand pieces of silver. [20] So mightily grew the word of God and prevailed.

11.1 Stay away from evil

Many persons will mix with evil and hope not to be affected. However, the Bible provides much guidance for persons to stay away from evil and the evil one.

Psalm 1:1-3

[1] Blessed is the man that walketh not in the counsel of the ungodly, nor standeth in the way of sinners, nor sitteth in the seat of the scornful. [2] But his delight is in the law of the LORD, and in his law doth he meditate day and night. [3] And he shall be like a tree planted by the rivers of water, that bringeth forth his fruit in his season; his leaf also shall not wither; and whatsoever he doeth shall prosper.

Those who walk in the path of the ungodly will be entrapped by the adversary. Satan plans to capture everyone and have them for himself, which is contrary to God's plan. Persons must resist Satan and accept the Lord.

James 4:7

[7] Submit yourselves therefore to God. Resist the devil, and he will flee from you.

11.2 Jesus delivered the demons from an unsound man

This man was demon-possessed. He lived in the tombs, and he was often seen naked. This man's actions would make any parent uncomfortable. Every parent would like to have their children delivered from demons.

Luke 8:26-39

[26] And they arrived at the country of the Gadarenes, which is over against Galilee. [27] And when he went forth to land, there met him out of the city a certain man, which had devils long time, and ware no

clothes, neither abode in any house, but in the tombs. 28 When he saw Jesus, he cried out, and fell before him, and with a loud voice said, What have I to do with thee, Jesus, thou Son of God most high? I beseech thee, torment me not. 29 (For he had commanded the unclean spirit to come out of the man. For oftentimes it had caught him: and he was kept bound with chains and in fetters; and he brake the bands, and was driven of the devil into the wilderness.)

30 And Jesus asked him, saying, What is thy name? And he said, Legion: because many devils were entered into him. 31 And they besought him that he would not command them to go out into the deep. 32 And there was there an herd of many swine feeding on the mountain: and they besought him that he would suffer them to enter into them. And he suffered them. 33 Then went the devils out of the man, and entered into the swine: and the herd ran violently down a steep place into the lake, and were choked. 34 When they that fed them saw what was done, they fled, and went and told it in the city and in the country.

35 Then they went out to see what was done; and came to Jesus, and found the man, out of whom the devils were departed, sitting at the feet of Jesus, clothed, and in his right mind: and they were afraid. 36 They also which saw it told them by what means he that was possessed of the devils was healed. 37 Then the whole multitude of the country of the Gadarenes round about besought him to depart from them; for they were taken with great fear: and he went up into the ship, and returned back again. 38 Now the man out of whom the devils were departed besought him that he might be with him: but Jesus sent him away, saying, 39 Return to thine own house, and shew how great things God hath done unto thee. And he went his way, and published throughout the whole city how great things Jesus had done unto him.

When demons are in people, it gives them extra power. In Luke 8:29, it tells us that the relatives of the man would chain him and hope that he would not escape, but he would break free from those chains and go to the wilderness. Nevertheless, Jesus was there to bring an end to the demons which made his life miserable.

The deliverance of that man who was possessed with demons brought joy to the hearts of his family. Before Jesus delivered the man, according to Luke 8:27, he was without clothes. However, after Jesus drove out the demons, he was clothed and sat at the feet of Jesus. Those who encounter the Lord and need deliverance can rest assured that once the Lord delivers them, they will be free. Who the Son of Man set free is free indeed.

The deliverance that the Lord has in store for everyone is instant. Therefore, once they come to the Lord in prayer, he is willing to deliver them immediately.

11.3 Deliverance from troubles

Many persons are faced with troubles, some of which they cannot resolve on their own. However, when they come to the Lord through prayer, he is willing to deliver them from their troubles.

Psalm 34:17-22

[17] The righteous cry, and the LORD heareth, and delivereth them out of all their troubles. [18] The LORD is nigh unto them that are of a broken heart; and saveth such as be of a contrite spirit. [19] Many are the afflictions of the righteous: but the LORD delivereth him out of them all. [20] He keepeth all his bones: not one of them is broken. [21] Evil shall slay the wicked: and they that hate the righteous shall be desolate. [22] The LORD redeemeth the soul of his servants: and none of them that trust in him shall be desolate.

The righteous are expected to pray to God for their deliverance. Psalm 107:6 tells us that the righteous cried unto the Lord and he delivered them.

Psalm 107:6

[6] Then they cried unto the LORD in their trouble, and he delivered them out of their distresses.

11.4 Deliverance from fears

Fear often affects the lives of individuals and causes them not to see their true potential. Fearful persons often do not want to engage in certain things, even if they have the ability, because they think they cannot do it or will fail to do that which is before them. However, the Lord wants to deliver all those who have fears.

Psalm 34:4-7

[4] I sought the LORD, and he heard me, and delivered me from all my fears. [5] They looked unto him, and were lightened: and their faces were not ashamed. [6] This poor man cried, and the LORD heard him, and saved him out of all his troubles. [7] The angel of the LORD encampeth round about them that fear him, and delivereth them.

Psalm 40:11-17

[11] Withhold not thou thy tender mercies from me, O LORD: let thy lovingkindness and thy truth continually preserve me. [12] For innumerable evils have compassed me about: mine iniquities have taken hold upon me, so that I am not able to look up; they are more than the hairs of mine head: therefore my heart faileth me. [13] Be pleased, O LORD, to deliver me: O LORD, make haste to help me. [14] Let them be ashamed and confounded together that seek after my soul to destroy it; let them be driven backward and put to shame that wish me evil. [15] Let them be desolate for a reward of their shame that say unto me, Aha, aha. [16] Let all those that seek thee rejoice and be glad in thee: let such as love thy salvation say continually, The LORD be magnified. [17] But I am poor and needy; yet the Lord thinketh upon me: thou art my help and my deliverer; make no tarrying, O my God.

11.5 Deliverance for all

It is God's intention that everyone will be delivered. Therefore, no one must keep their sickness, since there is hope for everyone. Those who are bound by demons will not be able to make positive contributions to their families and societies. Many times, when they plan something good, the demons will derail their plans.

2 Peter 2:9

[9] The Lord knoweth how to deliver the godly out of temptations, and to reserve the unjust unto the day of judgment to be punished.

12. Prayer for healing

Medical professionals are trained to help patients with their medical conditions. Oftentimes, persons will visit their doctors regularly for guidance and assistance. Doctors will use whatever resources they have at their disposal and training to help patients to improve their health. However, there are times when the medical condition a person is affected by cannot be healed by doctors. Doctors know their limitations and will inform their patients that their particular condition is beyond their capability.

But everyone has access to the healing that God has for them. If sinners seek the Lord, they can be healed. When Jesus died, he provided the opportunity for anyone who seeks Him to be healed. While Jesus walked on this earth, he was able to heal those who came to him; as a result, every human being all around the world gained access to his healing power after his death.

Isaiah 53:5

5 But he was wounded for our transgressions, he was bruised for our iniquities: the chastisement of our peace was upon him; and with his stripes we are healed.

Even before Jesus came to the earth in flesh, persons were already informed that by his stripes they would be healed. Therefore, the death of Jesus was essential so that he would receive those cruel stripes and those who seek healing from him will be healed. Sadly, one person had to be hurt so that others will live. However, Jesus was obedient unto death so that those who seek healing will find it.

12.1 Let the elders pray for the sick

The apostle James provides a reminder that if anyone is sick among the brethren, that person can call for the believers to pray for them. This reminds every believer that they have work to do for the kingdom of God. They can expect that people will approach them for prayer for whatever sickness is affecting them. Once the believers pray with their whole heart, then God will heal the sick.

James 5:13-16

13 Is any among you afflicted? let him pray. Is any merry? let him sing psalms. 14 Is any sick among you? let him call for the elders of the church; and let them pray over him, anointing him with oil in the name of the Lord: 15 And the prayer of faith shall save the sick, and the Lord shall raise him, and if he has committed sins, they shall be forgiven him. 16 Confess your faults one to another, and pray one for another, that ye may be healed. The effectual fervent prayer of a righteous man availeth much.

12.2 Jesus healed those who sought his help

Jesus is always willing to heal those who seek him. He is well aware that people need help, and he is willing to stretch out his hand to heal them. This is why he is called the Great Physician.

Luke 9:10-11

10 And the apostles, when they were returned, told him all that they had done. And he took them, and went aside privately into a desert place belonging to the city called Bethsaida. 11 And the people, when they knew it, followed him: and he received them, and spake unto them of the kingdom of God, and healed them that had need of healing.

12.3 Everyone can pray for their healing

Too often, persons depend on others to pray for their healing. Each person must establish a relationship with the Lord and seek God for their healing. There is no magic in seeking God for his healing.

Matthew 15:22-29

22 And, behold, a woman of Canaan came out of the same coasts, and cried unto him, saying, Have mercy on me, O Lord, thou son of David;

my daughter is grievously vexed with a devil. 23 But he answered her not a word. And his disciples came and besought him, saying, Send her away; for she crieth after us. 24 But he answered and said, I am not sent but unto the lost sheep of the house of Israel. 25 Then came she and worshipped him, saying, Lord, help me. 26 But he answered and said, It is not meet to take the children's bread, and to cast it to dogs. 27 And she said, Truth, Lord: yet the dogs eat of the crumbs which fall from their masters' table. 28 Then Jesus answered and said unto her, O woman, great is thy faith: be it unto thee even as thou wilt. And her daughter was made whole from that very hour. 29 And Jesus departed from thence, and came nigh unto the sea of Galilee; and went up into a mountain, and sat down there.

Healing is the children's bread. Since it is essential, God wants everyone to request their healing. Take note, the Canaanite woman knew that she was not entitled to certain blessings like the Jews. However, she approached Jesus anyway, because she wanted her daughter to be made whole. When Jesus answered her, she was willing to respond by acknowledging that she was not entitled to such blessing, but she still wanted him to have mercy on her. It is through her faith that her daughter was made whole.

Persons must be persistent with God and seek him until they are blessed. They must know that God is merciful and well able to heal them, but they must exercise their faith. Those who want to be healed cannot sit and do nothing and expect that God will reach them at their point of need. Faith, not fear, moves God. Therefore, every believer must let their faith arise and see God healing them and their families. They must approach God, expecting that he will heal them. As long as they do not waver in their faith, they can ask anything and see God working on their behalf.

12.4 God added more years to the king

When persons pray, they expect that God will only heal them and keep them healed for a short period. The duration of how long a person lives after their healing is all dependent on God.

When King Hezekiah was sick, he prayed, and God added fifteen more years to him. If the king had chosen not to pray and seek God for his healing, then he would have remained in the same position and would have died sooner.

Everyone who needs healing must be willing to approach God and hear from him. God is compassionate and willing to forgive persons of their sins, but they must seek him for their healing.

Take note in 2 Kings 20:1, it was the word of the Lord to Hezekiah, through the prophet Isaiah, that King Hezekiah would die. Therefore, this was a sure word. However, the king was not willing to accept that report, as he wanted to live and continue his reign over the kingdom. King Hezekiah's response was strange, but it was rewarding. Many persons would accept the word of the Lord through a prophet. However, King Hezekiah was not willing to accept God's word to him that he was going to die.

2 Kings 20:1-11

[1] In those days was Hezekiah sick unto death. And the prophet Isaiah the son of Amoz came to him, and said unto him, Thus saith the LORD, Set thine house in order; for thou shalt die, and not live. [2] Then he turned his face to the wall, and prayed unto the LORD, saying, [3] I beseech thee, O LORD, remember now how I have walked before thee in truth and with a perfect heart, and have done that which is good in thy sight. And Hezekiah wept sore. [4] And it came to pass, afore Isaiah was gone out into the middle court, that the word of the LORD came to him, saying, [5] Turn again, and tell Hezekiah the captain of my people, Thus saith the LORD, the God of David thy father, I have heard thy prayer, I have seen thy tears: behold, I will heal thee: on the third day thou shalt go up unto the house of the LORD. [6] And I will add unto thy days fifteen years; and I will deliver thee and this city out of the hand of the king of Assyria; and I will defend this city for mine own sake, and for my servant David's sake.

[7] And Isaiah said, Take a lump of figs. And they took and laid it on the boil, and he recovered. [8] And Hezekiah said unto Isaiah, What shall be the sign that the LORD will heal me, and that I shall go up into the house of the LORD the third day? [9] And Isaiah said, This sign shalt thou have of the LORD, that the LORD will do the thing that he hath spoken: shall the shadow go forward ten degrees, or go back ten degrees? [10] And Hezekiah answered, It is a light thing for the shadow to go down ten degrees: nay, but let the shadow return backward ten degrees. [11] And Isaiah the prophet cried unto the LORD: and he

brought the shadow ten degrees backward, by which it had gone down in the dial of Ahaz.

Believers must know that Isaiah was not a false prophet. Isaiah was only working with the instruction of the Lord. The thing that changed God's response toward King Hezekiah was Hezekiah's prayer. Therefore, every believer must know that their prayer is powerful and God will listen to their prayers. There is no separation or status when it comes to God, since he is willing to listen to those of low status and high status alike. Once persons pray from a clean heart, then God will listen to them.

Many more persons must take a similar approach to King Hezekiah and pray unto God for their healing. They must remind God of his commitment to them. They must live a life that pleases God, so when they remind God of their deeds, he will agree with them.

13. Prayer changes barrenness

Most women desire to become a mother, as they would like to have a generation following them. But many women are suffering from physical barrenness, unable to conceive a child.

When women are barren, they receive harsh criticism from persons that they know. On many occasions, those women have not done anything to cause themselves to be barren, yet they are condemned.

Figure 15. Who causes barrenness?

People

- It happens because of people's actions or inactions. Health issues are another factor to consider.

God

- It happens because he wants it to be so.

Some women are affected by health issues that affect their ability to become pregnant. Men can also be affected by infertility that prevents them from producing fertile sperm. People are also reminded to stay healthy. They ought to engage in exercising and eating healthy food that will help their bodies to become nourished.

When some persons are barren, they blame their partners. Blaming one's partner is a very serious issue that can often cause many conflicts within the family. Both persons must visit their gynecologist for medical advice. If a person is not satisfied with the views of one gynecologist, then they can visit another medical practitioner for advice.

However, despite all of man's efforts and professional medical support, some persons remain barren. This may cause those persons to turn to God for help. This is the best option available when no human can help.

Sometimes, people have to inquire if it is God who has caused them to be barren for some time. Consider Abraham and Sarah. There were living together, and it took them many years, through a period of barrenness, before they had a child. What was also noticeable about God's intervention in their situation is that they were both senior-aged persons when God removed the temporary barrenness from them.

13.1 Hannah became pregnant

There is another familiar woman in the Bible who was barren. Her name is Hannah, and her story is well known to many believers. What is very interesting in this story is that it was God who had shut up her womb. Her husband had children with his other wife, Peninnah, but Hannah was barren.

However, what God was doing in her life was very significant, and she produced a son, Samuel, who became one of the important prophets in the Bible. People need to know that God's delay often happens for some significant purpose.

1 Samuel 1:9-21

9 So Hannah rose up after they had eaten in Shiloh, and after they had drunk. Now Eli the priest sat upon a seat by a post of the temple of the LORD. 10 And she was in bitterness of soul, and prayed unto the LORD, and wept sore. 11 And she vowed a vow, and said, O LORD of hosts, if thou wilt indeed look on the affliction of thine handmaid, and remember me, and not forget thine handmaid, but wilt give unto thine handmaid a man child, then I will give him unto the LORD all the days of his life, and there shall no razor come upon his head.

12 And it came to pass, as she continued praying before the LORD, that Eli marked her mouth. 13 Now Hannah, she spake in her heart; only her lips moved, but her voice was not heard: therefore Eli thought she had been drunken. 14 And Eli said unto her, How long wilt thou be drunken? put away thy wine from thee. 15 And Hannah answered and said, No, my lord, I am a woman of a sorrowful spirit:

I have drunk neither wine nor strong drink, but have poured out my soul before the LORD. [16] Count not thine handmaid for a daughter of Belial: for out of the abundance of my complaint and grief have I spoken hitherto. [17] Then Eli answered and said, Go in peace: and the God of Israel grant thee thy petition that thou hast asked of him. [18] And she said, Let thine handmaid find grace in thy sight. So the woman went her way, and did eat, and her countenance was no more sad.

[19] And they rose up in the morning early, and worshipped before the LORD, and returned, and came to their house to Ramah: and Elkanah knew Hannah his wife; and the LORD remembered her. [20] Wherefore it came to pass, when the time was come about after Hannah had conceived, that she bare a son, and called his name Samuel, saying, Because I have asked him of the LORD. [21] And the man Elkanah, and all his house, went up to offer unto the LORD the yearly sacrifice, and his vow.

According to 1 Samuel 1:9-21, it was God who shut up Hannah's womb. However, Hannah made her situation a matter of prayer. What is important to know is that she did not accept that she would remain barren while her husband had children with another woman. She was desperate, and she sought God's intervention.

Every believer must share her passion to pursue God. Do not accept certain conditions, but make your request known unto God.

Hannah did not only pray unto God, but she was willing to make a covenant with God. She raised her intensity and was willing to do something different, as she needed God to give her a breakthrough.

When prayers are normal and no effort is placed into them, the results will be normal. However, when prayers are intense and made unto God, persons can look forward to a favorable result. Never quit on your prayers to God, since only he has the answer to your prayer.

Hannah's prayer moved God to respond in her favor. She was not willing to leave the presence of God until God blessed her. Her persistent approach was similar to Jacob, who wrestled with the angel.

God is willing to work on his children's behalf, but he wants his children to approach him as a Father who has control over the universe. He is not short of anything and always wants to bless his children.

Prayer is one thing that believers can use to get God's attention. It is known that God will listen to the sinners when they pray.

1 John 1:6-10

[6] If we say that we have fellowship with him, and walk in darkness, we lie, and do not the truth: [7] But if we walk in the light, as he is in the light, we have fellowship one with another, and the blood of Jesus Christ his Son cleanseth us from all sin. [8] If we say that we have no sin, we deceive ourselves, and the truth is not in us. [9] If we confess our sins, he is faithful and just to forgive us our sins, and to cleanse us from all unrighteousness. [10] If we say that we have not sinned, we make him a liar, and his word is not in us.

It is God's intention that sinners should confess their sins and seek him. He will forgive them, listen to them, and bless them. God's mercy extends to all humanity.

13.2 Rebekah became pregnant

In the passage below, Genesis 25:1-26, Jacob was forty years old when he married Rebekah, but it took them another twenty years before they had their first child. This was temporary barrenness, but Jacob prayed unto God and his prayers were answered.

Genesis 25:19-26

[19] And these are the generations of Isaac, Abraham's son: Abraham begat Isaac: [20] And Isaac was forty years old when he took Rebekah to wife, the daughter of Bethuel the Syrian of Padanaram, the sister to Laban the Syrian. [21] And Isaac intreated the LORD for his wife, because she was barren: and the LORD was intreated of him, and Rebekah his wife conceived. [22] And the children struggled together within her; and she said, If it be so, why am I thus? And she went to enquire of the LORD. [23] And the LORD said unto her, Two nations are in thy womb, and two manner of people shall be separated from thy bowels; and the one people shall be stronger than the other people; and the elder shall serve the younger. [24] And when her days to be delivered were fulfilled, behold, there were twins in her womb. [25] And the first came out red, all over like an hairy garment; and they called his name Esau. [26] And

after that came his brother out, and his hand took hold on Esau's heel; and his name was called Jacob: and Isaac was threescore years old when she bare them.

The scripture above is very interesting, since God used one of Isaac's offspring to be a part of the lineage into which Jesus was born. If Jacob had accepted that he and his wife would remain barren, then their names would have not been mentioned in scripture unto today.

No one must accept defeat when God is available to them. There may be some temporary delays, but if they follow God with their prayers, they can expect to have their breakthrough.

13.3 God has promised to make his children fruitful

In Deuteronomy 7:11-16, God made a covenant with his children to bless them. He was willing to bless their animals and their lands. Therefore, God intends to bless his children and their possessions and not to make them barren, as he states in Deuteronomy 7:14. Therefore, every believer can approach God for his blessings over their lives and change their barren state to a state of fruitfulness.

Deuteronomy 7:11-16

11 Thou shalt therefore keep the commandments, and the statutes, and the judgments, which I command thee this day, to do them. 12 Wherefore it shall come to pass, if ye hearken to these judgments, and keep, and do them, that the LORD thy God shall keep unto thee the covenant and the mercy which he sware unto thy fathers: 13 And he will love thee, and bless thee, and multiply thee: he will also bless the fruit of thy womb, and the fruit of thy land, thy corn, and thy wine, and thine oil, the increase of thy kine, and the flocks of thy sheep, in the land which he sware unto thy fathers to give thee. 14 Thou shalt be blessed above all people: there shall not be male or female barren among you, or among your cattle. 15 And the LORD will take away from thee all sickness, and will put none of the evil diseases of Egypt, which thou knowest, upon thee; but will lay them upon all them that hate thee. 16 And thou shalt consume all the people which the LORD thy God shall deliver thee; thine eye shall have no pity upon them: neither shalt thou serve their gods; for that will be a snare unto thee.

13.4 Elizabeth became pregnant in her old age

Just as Sarah became pregnant in her senior years, a similar thing happened to Elizabeth. She might have thought that her days of pregnancy were over, but God had the final say. He was willing to change her barrenness to fruitfulness, and Elizabeth gave birth to John the Baptist.

As persons pray and trust God, he will do wonders for them. Elizabeth moved from barrenness to being a mother whose son was the forerunner of Jesus.

Luke 1:34-38

34 Then said Mary unto the angel, How shall this be, seeing I know not a man? 35 And the angel answered and said unto her, The Holy Ghost shall come upon thee, and the power of the Highest shall overshadow thee: therefore also that holy thing which shall be born of thee shall be called the Son of God. 36 And, behold, thy cousin Elisabeth, she hath also conceived a son in her old age: and this is the sixth month with her, who was called barren. 37 For with God nothing shall be impossible. 38 And Mary said, Behold the handmaid of the Lord; be it unto me according to thy word. And the angel departed from her.

14. Prayer for enlarged borders

God wants to enlarge the borders for all believers. While many believers operate at only one stage, God intends to allow them to progress. Every believer must have more and more influence around the world. What they can do today must be better than what they were able to do within the last decade.

The influence of believers must also go beyond their house, community, or country. Every believer can impact the world. However, to be ready to impact the world, believers must stay connected with God. They must also ask him to enlarge their borders.

It is Christ who called believers to go as far as possible to share his Good News. He gave every believer a Great Commission to spread his gospel. This now gives believers opportunities to take the gospel as far as possible. Therefore, if believers will take the gospel far and wide, they must also ask God to enlarge their borders.

Too many believers are comfortable sitting within the church and working from that one small location. However, there are more people beyond that location for them to reach and share the Good News. In Matthew 28:18, Jesus immediately greeted the believers and reminded them that all power is given unto them. Therefore, as they go forth doing his work, they must know that they are not powerless, but powerful.

Matthew 28:18-20

18 And Jesus came and spake unto them, saying, All power is given unto me in heaven and in earth. 19 Go ye therefore, and teach all nations, baptizing them in the name of the Father, and of the Son, and of the Holy Ghost: 20 Teaching them to observe all things whatsoever I have commanded you: and, lo, I am with you always, even unto the end of the world. Amen.

14.1 Preach and teach at all times

Those who have prayed and received the authority from God to go and share his word must keep praying and continue his work. When others go to share God's word, those who are unable to go must spend time in prayer. Working in the field to win souls is not easy. It also requires that persons pray for them and encourage them as they labor for the Lord.

2 Timothy 4:1-6

[1] I charge thee therefore before God, and the Lord Jesus Christ, who shall judge the quick and the dead at his appearing and his kingdom; [2] Preach the word; be instant in season, out of season; reprove, rebuke, exhort with all long suffering and doctrine. [3] For the time will come when they will not endure sound doctrine; but after their own lusts shall they heap to themselves teachers, having itching ears; [4] And they shall turn away their ears from the truth, and shall be turned unto fables. [5] But watch thou in all things, endure afflictions, do the work of an evangelist, make full proof of thy ministry. [6] For I am now ready to be offered, and the time of my departure is at hand.

14.2 Pray for those who go forth to spread the gospel

In Paul's writing in 2 Thessalonians 3, he reminded the brethren to pray for them. This is very true, since when believers are doing the works of the Lord, they are constantly under attack. No one doing the works of the Lord is free from trouble. While they will not be looking for trouble, it will come their way.

2 Thessalonians 3:1-5

[1] Finally, brethren, pray for us, that the word of the Lord may have free course, and be glorified, even as it is with you: [2] And that we may be delivered from unreasonable and wicked men: for all men have not faith. [3] But the Lord is faithful, who shall establish you, and keep you from evil. [4] And we have confidence in the Lord touching you, that ye both do and will do the things which we command you. [5] And the Lord direct your hearts into the love of God, and into the patient waiting for Christ.

At some churches, there is an evangelism team and an intercessory team. These two teams work in tandem: the intercessors will constantly pray for the evangelism team, so that the word of the Lord will reach many persons and change sinners' hearts. The gospel must be spread, so someone must be willing to share the gospel as far as possible.

Every church must remain prayerful and ask God for opportunities to expand his Kingdom through them. Even when they do not have all the finances they need, they must make it a matter of prayer.

Too many souls need to hear the word of the Lord, and sometimes, there are too few persons to spread the Good News. There, you have a great opportunity to pray for God to send more laborers. As God sends more laborers, pray that they will make a great impact wherever they go.

Jesus sent his followers out, two by two. He wanted them to share his Good News. Jesus asked them to pray that God would send laborers to the harvest. Every believer must also constantly pray that God will send more laborers to the harvest.

Luke 10:1-20

1 After these things the LORD appointed other seventy also, and sent them two and two before his face into every city and place, whither he himself would come. 2 Therefore said he unto them, The harvest truly is great, but the labourers are few: pray ye therefore the Lord of the harvest, that he would send forth labourers into his harvest. 3 Go your ways: behold, I send you forth as lambs among wolves. 4 Carry neither purse, nor scrip, nor shoes: and salute no man by the way. 5 And into whatsoever house ye enter, first say, Peace be to this house. 6 And if the son of peace be there, your peace shall rest upon it: if not, it shall turn to you again. 7 And in the same house remain, eating and drinking such things as they give: for the labourer is worthy of his hire. Go not from house to house.

8 And into whatsoever city ye enter, and they receive you, eat such things as are set before you: 9 And heal the sick that are therein, and say unto them, The kingdom of God is come nigh unto you. 10 But into whatsoever city ye enter, and they receive you not, go your ways out into the streets of the same, and say, 11 Even the very dust of your city, which cleaveth on us, we do wipe off against you:

notwithstanding be ye sure of this, that the kingdom of God comes nigh unto you.

¹² But I say unto you, that it shall be more tolerable in that day for Sodom, than for that city. ¹³ Woe unto thee, Chorazin! woe unto thee, Bethsaida! for if the mighty works had been done in Tyre and Sidon, which have been done in you, they had a great while ago repented, sitting in sackcloth and ashes. ¹⁴ But it shall be more tolerable for Tyre and Sidon at the judgment, than for you. ¹⁵ And thou, Capernaum, which art exalted to heaven, shalt be thrust down to hell. ¹⁶ He that heareth you heareth me; and he that despiseth you despiseth me; and he that despiseth me despiseth him that sent me.

¹⁷ And the seventy returned again with joy, saying, Lord, even the devils are subject unto us through thy name. ¹⁸ And he said unto them, I beheld Satan as lightning fall from heaven. ¹⁹ Behold, I give unto you power to tread on serpents and scorpions, and over all the power of the enemy: and nothing shall by any means hurt you. ²⁰ Notwithstanding in this rejoice not, that the spirits are subject unto you; but rather rejoice, because your names are written in heaven.

14.3 Jabez prayed

God's word provide believers with an example of Jabez who prayed for his coast to be enlarged. This ought to be a similar prayer for many believers. Some believers are comfortable with the things which they are doing, but they need to reach beyond their current space. Jabez also wanted God to watch over him and keep him from evil. When Jabez prayed, God granted his request. It must be known, that God listens to the prayer of his children.

1 Chronicles 4:9-10

⁹ And Jabez was more honourable than his brethren: and his mother called his name Jabez, saying, Because I bare him with sorrow. ¹⁰ And Jabez called on the God of Israel, saying, Oh that thou wouldest bless me indeed, and enlarge my coast, and that thine hand might be with me, and that thou wouldest keep me from evil, that it may not grieve me! And God granted him that which he requested.

Do not live your life as though prayer is optional; rather, live your life as though prayer is your only choice, especially if you want to see the hands-on

God in a mighty way. When persons cease to pray, it is almost as though they are ceasing to breathe. Since breathing is essential to living, so too is prayer essential for the believer's success. The Bible says that "men ought always to pray, and not to faint" (Luke 18:1).

About the author

All of the books written by author Geary Reid became possible because of his relationship with God. He constantly prays and seeks God's wisdom in writing these books, and God often responds favorably. He knows how important prayer is, so he starts his day with prayer. Whenever he has challenges, he makes it a matter of prayer. Before he consumes his food, he also prays for the meal provided. When he enters his vehicle, he prays.

One of the ministries he has been a part of within the church is the intercessory ministry. On many occasions, he is called upon to pray for various things. He is not ashamed to pray whenever he is requested to, whether it is in private or at public events. Even at his place of employment, when persons ask him to pray with them, he does so joyfully.

Just as Jesus treats prayer as an important thing, Reid wants to remind all believers to make prayer a priority. When he was called to serve God in 1986, he knew that he had to strengthen his walk with the Lord through prayer. Since those days, he has worked towards intensifying his prayer life. During his many years of prayer, he has seen many great things happen, and he is constantly looking to God for more victories for many persons.

Reid has many testimonies about prayer. He has seen God cause persons who were barren to give birth. On many occasions, when he is going somewhere and it rains, he will ask God to cease the rain within a short period, and God has often granted his request.

If believers spend more time in prayer and less time complaining, then their lives will become more impactful. Persons must not wait until they reach the church building to pray; they must have a quality private prayer life. This is something that Geary Reid would like to see more believers do immediately.

Your prayers matter. So pray and pray, and God will give you the victory.